PROJECT 2003

PERSONAL TRAINER

PROJECT 2003
PERSONAL TRAINER

CustomGuide, Inc.

O'REILLY®

Beijing • Cambridge • Farnham • Köln • Paris • Sebastopol • Taipei • Tokyo

Project 2003 Personal Trainer
by CustomGuide, Inc.

Published by O'Reilly Media, Inc., 1005 Gravenstein Highway North, Sebastopol, CA 95472.

O'Reilly books may be purchased for educational, business, or sales promotional use. Online editions are also available for most titles (*safari.oreilly.com*). For more information, contact our corporate/institutional sales department: (800) 998-9938 or *corporate@oreilly.com*.

Editor	Michele Filshie
Production Editor	Genevieve d'Entremont
Art Director	Michele Wetherbee
Cover Designer	Emma Colby
Cover Illustrator	Brian Kong
Interior Designer	Melanie Wang

Printing History

June 2005:   First Edition.

RepKover™ This book uses RepKover™, a durable and flexible lay-flat binding.

ISBN: 0-596-00854-6
[C]

CONTENTS

Contents

About CustomGuide, Inc.

CustomGuide, Inc. (*http://www.customguide.com*) is a leading provider of training materials and e-learning for organizations; their client list includes Harvard, Yale, and Oxford universities. CustomGuide was founded by a small group of instructors who were dissatisfied by the dry and technical nature of computer training materials available to trainers and educators. They decided to write their own series of courseware that would be fun and user-friendly; and best of all, they would license it in electronic format so instructors could print only the topics they needed for a class or training session. Later, they found themselves unhappy with the e-learning industry and decided to create a new series of online, interactive training that matched their courseware. Today employees, students, and instructors at more than 2,000 organizations worldwide use CustomGuide courseware to help teach and learn about computers.

CustomGuide, Inc. Staff and Contributors

Jonathan High	President	Jeremy Weaver	Senior Programmer
Daniel High	Vice President of Sales and Marketing	Luke Davidson	Programmer
		Lisa Price	Director of Business Development
Melissa Peterson	Senior Writer/Editor	Megan Diemand	Office Manager and Sales Representative
Kitty Rogers	Writer/Editor		
Stephen Meinz	Writer/Editor	Soda Rajsombath	Sales Representative
Stan Keathly	Senior Developer	Hallie Stork	Sales Representative
Jeffrey High	Developer	Sarah Saeger	Sales Support
Chris Kanneman	Developer	Julie Geisler	Narrator

INTRODUCTION

About the Personal Trainer Series

Most software manuals are as hard to navigate as the programs they describe. They assume that you're going to read all 500 pages from start to finish, and that you can gain intimate familiarity with the program simply by reading about it. Some books give you sample files to practice on, but when you're finding your way around a new set of skills, it's all too easy to mess up program settings or delete data files and not know how to recover. Even if William Shakespeare and Bill Gates teamed up to write a book about Microsoft Project, their book would be frustrating to read because most people learn by doing the task.

While we don't claim to be rivals to either Bill, we think we have a winning formula in the Personal Trainer series. We've created a set of lessons that reflect the tasks you really want to do, whether as simple as resizing or as complex as integrating multimedia components. Each lesson breaks a task into a series of simple steps, showing you exactly what to do to accomplish the task.

And instead of leaving you hanging, the interactive CD in the back of this book recreates the application for you to experiment in. In our unique simulator, there's no worry about permanently damaging your preferences, turning all your documents purple, losing data, or any of the other things that can go wrong when you're testing your new skills in the unforgiving world of the real application. It's fully interactive, giving you feedback and guidance as you work through the exercises—just like a real trainer!

Our friendly guides can improve your skills in record time. You'll learn the secrets of the professionals in a safe environment, with exercises and homework for those of you who really want to break the pain barrier. You'll have your Project 2003 skills in shape in no time!

About This Book

We've aimed this book at Miscrosoft Project 2003. Some features may look different or simply not exist if you're using another version of the program. If our simulator doesn't match your application, check the version number to make sure you're using the right version.

Since this is a hands-on course, each lesson contains an exercise with step-by-step instructions for you to follow.

To make learning easier, every exercise follows certain conventions:

- This book never assumes you know where (or what) something is. The first time you're told to click something, a picture of what you're supposed to click appears in the illustrations at the beginning of the lesson.

- When you see a keyboard instruction like "press Ctrl + B," you should press and hold the first key (Ctrl in this example) while you press the second key (B in this example). Then, after you've pressed both keys, you can release them.

Our exclusive Quick Reference box appears at the end of every lesson. You can use it to review the skills you've learned in the lesson and as a handy reference—when you need to know how to do something fast and don't need to step through the entire exercise.

Conventions Used in This Book

The following is a list of typographical conventions used in this book:

Italic

Shows important terms the first time they are presented.

`Constant Width`

Shows anything you're supposed to type.

Color

Shows anything you're supposed to click, drag, or press.

 NOTE *Warns you of pitfalls that you could encounter if you're not careful.*

TIP *Indicates a suggestion or supplementary information to the topic at hand.*

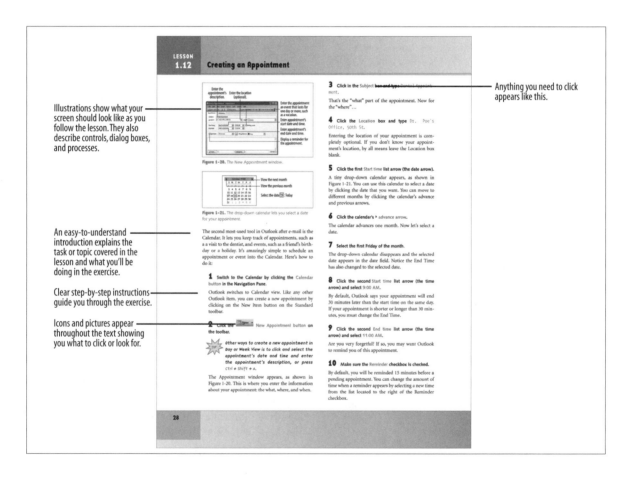

Illustrations show what your screen should look like as you follow the lesson. They also describe controls, dialog boxes, and processes.

An easy-to-understand introduction explains the task or topic covered in the lesson and what you'll be doing in the exercise.

Clear step-by-step instructions guide you through the exercise.

Icons and pictures appear throughout the text showing you what to click or look for.

Anything you need to click appears like this.

Using the Interactive Environment

Minimum Specs

- Windows 98 or better
- 64 MB RAM
- 150 MB Disk Space

Installation Instructions

Insert disc into CD-ROM drive. Click the "Install" button at the prompt. The installer will give you the option of installing the "Interactive Content" and the "Practice Files." These are both installed by default. Practice files are also included on the CD in a directory called "Practice Files," which can be accessed without installing anything. If you select the installation item, the installer will then create a shortcut in your Start menu under the title "Personal Trainer," which you can use to access your installation selections.

Use of Interactive Content

Once you've installed the interactive content, placing the disc in your drive will cause the program to launch automatically. Then, once it has launched, just make your lesson selections and learn away!

How to Contact Us

We have tested and verified the information in this book to the best of our ability, but you might find that features have changed (or even that we have made mistakes!). As a reader of this book, you can help us to improve future editions by sending us your feedback. Please let us know about any errors, inaccuracies, bugs, misleading or confusing statements, and typos that you find anywhere in this book.

Please also let us know what we can do to make this book more useful to you. We take your comments seriously and will try to incorporate reasonable suggestions into future editions. You can write to us at:

O'Reilly Media, Inc.
1005 Gravenstein Highway North
Sebastopol, CA 95472

800) 998-9938 (in the U.S. or Canada)
(707) 829-0515 (international or local)
(707) 829-0104 (fax)

To ask technical questions or to comment on the book, send email to:

bookquestions@oreilly.com

The web site for *Microsoft Project 2003 Personal Trainer* lists examples, errata, and plans for future editions. You can find this page at:

http://www.oreilly.com/catalog/projectpt

For more information about this book and others, see the O'Reilly web site at:

http://www.oreilly.com

Safari® Enabled

When you see a Safari® Enabled icon on the cover of your favorite technology book, that means the book is available online through the O'Reilly Network Safari Bookshelf.

Safari offers a solution that's better than e-books. It's a virtual library that lets you easily search thousands of top tech books, cut and paste code samples, download chapters, and find quick answers when you need the most accurate, current information. Try it for free at *http://safari.oreilly.com*.

THE FUNDAMENTALS

CHAPTER OBJECTIVES:

Plan the project and understand project management, Lessons 1.1 and 1.2

See what's new in Microsoft Project 2003, Lesson 1.3

Understand the Project 2003 screen, Lesson 1.4

Use Project's views, Lessons 1.5 and 1.6

Create a new Project file, Lesson 1.7

Enter project information, Lessons 1.8 and 1.9

Set the working time calendar, Lessons 1.10 and 1.11

Create a new base calendar, Lesson 1.12

Use the Project Guide, Lesson 1.13

Print the project, Lessons 1.14 and 1.15

Use Help, Lesson 1.16

Prerequisites

- **Project Standard or Professional 2003 installed on your computer.**
- **Basic computer knowledge.**

Welcome to your first chapter on Microsoft Project 2003! Project 2003 is a high-powered project management tool that you can use to control and track any kind of project once it has been planned. With Project 2003, you can see every detail of your project simultaneously so you can follow its progress.

For years, people have been completing projects, like mailing Christmas cards or building a ten-ton steel bridge, without the aid of software. So why use project management software? The answer is simple: because your project will be completed as painlessly and problem-free as possible.

Project 2003 can be a bit intimidating at first, with its big, blank default screen and its many buttons and views. But don't worry; this chapter will introduce you to some of the basic functions of Project 2003. Also, if you've already used more basic Microsoft applications, such as Word, you'll already know how to perform many simple Project 2003 tasks. With that in mind, this chapter is your introduction to Microsoft Project 2003 and the world of project management. And so, without further ado, turn the page and let's get started!

Planning the Project

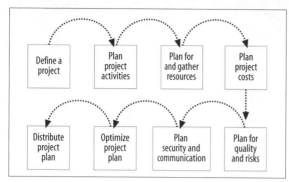

Figure 1-1. Steps in planning a project.

Perhaps the most difficult step in Project 2003 is the first one: planning the project. Planning requires constant research and editing. In fact, you may find that the planning stage of a project doesn't really end until you're finished with the project.

So how can you prepare yourself, and what can you do to make this process pain-free? The illustration in Figure 1-1 shows a common progression of steps to take when planning a project, depending on the type of project you're tackling. Table 1-1 describes these steps in further detail. It is important to note, however, that these steps are merely guidelines for planning a project and will change depending on the type of project you are doing.

Table 1-1. Planning Steps

Step	Description
Define a project	**Initiate the project:** Clearly identify the purpose and goals of the project; estimate when key resources will be available to work on the project; make backup plans for key project components; and identify the project's constraints and limitations, such as the schedule, resources, budget, and scope.
	Start a project file: Create the project's file and set the project's properties, such as working time (i.e., Monday through Friday, 8 a.m. to 5 p.m.).
	Define project deliverables: Define the actual product or service that meets the project's objectives.
Plan project activities	**Define phases and create a task list:** Enter the tasks required to complete the project, define the project's phases, and add any supporting information to the task.
	Show the project's organization: Structure the tasks into their respective phases, and create a hierarchy of summary tasks and subtasks.
	Organize the project into master project and subproject files: Complete a large project (master project) by completing smaller projects (subprojects).
	Estimate task duration: Estimate how long a task will take to complete, considering nonworking time. Fine-tune duration with the Task Calendar.
	Set task dependencies and constraints: Identify and link tasks that affect the progress of another task.
	Create interrelationships with projects: Identify tasks in the master project that are dependent upon tasks in subprojects.
Plan for and gather resources	**Estimate resource needs:** Compile a list of all the resources you will need, and change the project duration as necessary. Also get input from others involved in the project.
	Enter resource information and set working times: Update information about the resources, and set the hours they will work.
	Share resources among projects: Sharing resources can help make it easier to manage a project's progress.
	Assign resources to tasks: Assign resources to specific tasks and the amount of time they are expected to work on the task.

Table 1-1. Planning Steps (Continued)

Step	Description
Plan project costs	**Estimate costs:** Research previous projects to estimate how much a task will cost. **Define and share cost information:** Prepare a budget, establish a baseline plan, and share the information with the parties involved. **Prepare to manage costs:** Set a fiscal year for the project, plan how to track and manage costs, and track the cash-flow plan.
Plan for quality and risks	**Plan for quality:** Define quality standards and determine how quality affects the overall scope of the project. **Identify and plan for risks:** Research reliable resources, identify risks, and create a plan of action to handle risk events should they occur.
Plan security and communication	**Set up methods for communicating project information:** Decide and establish a procedure for how you want to share project information with everyone involved. **Protect project information:** Depending on the communication resource you use, set passwords, specify security settings, etc.
Optimize a project plan	Optimize the project plan to meet the finish date, plan for resources, and complete the project within its budget constraints.
Distribute a project plan	Depending on how you share and communicate the project's information, distribute the project's plan online or in printed format.

Remember, you still have to plan the project yourself. Microsoft Project 2003 can only help you record and keep track of all the tasks, resources, and costs within it.

Understanding Project Management

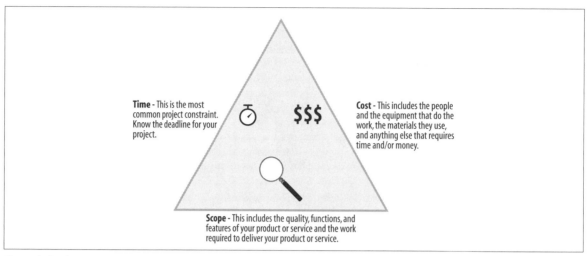

Figure 1-2. The Project Triangle.

We all basically know what a project is, but here is a clear definition: A *project* is a temporary series of actions undertaken to create a unique product or service. A project can be anything from building a fleet of helicopters, to planning a wedding, to writing a sushi cookbook. All projects have three things in common: (1) they have a start and end date, (2) they are an effort made by people and equipment, and (3) they create a product or service. You've probably already completed many projects and are working on many projects as we speak. That means you already have experience with project management.

Project management is the process of planning, organizing, and managing tasks and resources to accomplish an objective, usually within constraints of time, resources, or cost. Project management has been a recognized profession since the 1950s but has been practiced since the Stone Ages. Without project management, we would still be wearing animal hides and rubbing sticks together to make fire.

An easy way to visualize the elements of project management is by using the Project Triangle, as shown in Figure 1-2. The Project Triangle views project management in terms of time, cost, and scope.

- *Time* is the amount of time it will take you to complete your project.
- *Cost* is the amount of money and time you will spend on the project.
- *Scope* is the quality, functions, and features of your product or service.

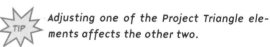 **Adjusting one of the Project Triangle elements affects the other two.**

To see what happens to project management when one side of the Project Triangle changes, see Table 1-2.

Table 1-2. If/Then in the Project Triangle

If	Then
If the project scope increases…	…then you may need more resources and/or additional time to do the extra work.
Example: If you decide you want to publish a definitive textbook instead of your original plan—a brief reference paperback…	…then either you find graduate students to help research the book, or you postpone the release of the book to allow time for the extra research.
If the time (duration) of your project schedule decreases…	…then you may need to increase cost (budget) in order to hire more resources to get everything done on time. If you can't increase the cost, you may need to reduce the scope, because it will be hard to get things done in less time.
Example: If you need to move your release date up two months in time for the new academic year…	…then either you recruit additional writers to contribute to the book, or you decide not to publish the book in hardcover.
If the cost (budget) of your project decreases…	…then you may need more time because you can't pay for as many resources. If you can't increase the time, you may need to reduce the scope, because fewer resources can't finish all of your planned work in the time you have scheduled.
Example: If the cost of one of the contributing authors puts you over your budget…	…then extend the deadline so another author can write the chapter, or leave out that chapter of the book.

The key to product management is keeping careful records and tracking your project. Microsoft Project 2003 will do that for you, so you can foresee any problems before they arise and adjust to changes accordingly.

QUICK REFERENCE

ALL PROJECTS:

- HAVE A START AND END DATE
- ARE EFFORTS MADE BY PEOPLE OR EQUIPMENT
- CREATE A PRODUCT OR SERVICE

THE PROJECT TRIANGLE INCLUDES:

- TIME
- COST
- SCOPE

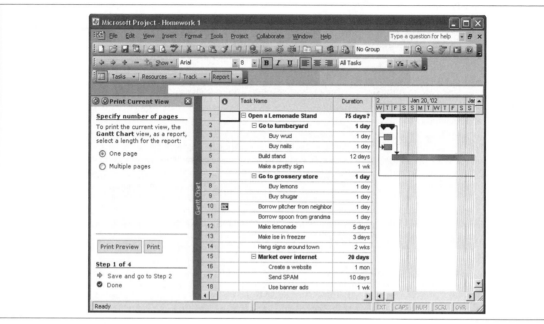

Figure 1-3. The Print Current View as a Report option is a new feature in Project 2003.

Before we start talking about new features of recent and past versions of the program, it helps if you actually understand what Project 2003 really is—a *database*. In its simplest form, a *database* is a collection of information that is organized into a list. Here is what a good database does:

- **Stores Information:** A database stores lists of information that are related to a particular subject or purpose. A database stores personal information, such as a list of Aunt Mildred's cookie recipes, or business information, such as a list of hundreds of thousands of resources. A database also makes it easy to add, update, organize, and delete information.

- **Finds Information:** You can easily and instantly locate information stored in a database. For example, you can find all the recipes in your cookbook with the ingredient "rice" in them or all your contractors located in the 58251 ZIP Code.

- **Analyzes Information:** You can perform calculations on information in a database. For example, you could

calculate what percent of your total equipment comes from the state of Texas. You can also present information in a professional-looking printed report.

- **Manages Information:** Databases make it easy to work with and manage huge amounts of information. For example, you can change the due date from 5/1/06 to 5/20/06 for hundreds of tasks with just a few keystrokes.

- **Shares Information:** Most database programs (including Microsoft Project 2003) allow more than one user to view and work with the same information at once. Such databases are called *multiuser databases*.

Project does all of these things, with the added bonus that it actually calculates information for scheduling the project. Table 1-3 lists some of the major additions to Project 2003, as well as new additions for users upgrading from Project 2000 or earlier.

Table 1-3. What's New in Project 2003?

Feature	Definition
New in 2003	
Print Current View as a Report	Print a view the way you want to in Project 2003, as shown in Figure 1-3. Click the Report button list arrow on the Project Guide toolbar to summon a wizard that will help guide you through the steps of printing a view as a report.
Copy Picture to Office Wizard	This feature allows you to display project data as a static picture in other applications, such as PowerPoint. This feature is found in the Analysis toolbar.
New in 2002	
Project Guide	This wizard-like feature appears in the left pane to help you build a new project, manage tasks and resources, specify and change working time, track your project, and report project information.
Smart Tags	These context-sensitive tags offer advice for alternative actions as you delete task or resource names and change resource assignments; start and finish dates; and work, units, or durations.
Task panes	The task pane appears on the left side of the screen and lets you quickly perform searches, open or start a new document, view the contents of the clipboard, or even access language translation and template services.
Improved views	Functionality has been added to the Network Diagram view and usage views (for example, including totals in a view). You can also display up to three timescales in some views.
Integrated with other programs	Project is XML-compatible so you can import, export, and save files in XML format. Easily import data from Microsoft Excel and export data back to Excel, and import/export other supported file types. Project managers can use the Excel Task List template to start their task lists. They can then import this Excel file into Microsoft Project smoothly, without having to map any fields. Easily import a task list from Microsoft Outlook into Microsoft Project.
Improved collaboration features	New features, such as the new Collaboration menu, make it easier to access, manage, and use collaborative projects.

Don't worry if you don't understand all of these features; Table 1-3 is a lot of tech-speak! What's important is that you learn how to use the program. That said, let's get going…

Understanding the Project 2003 Screen

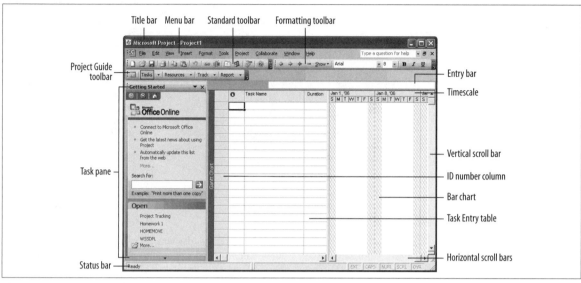

Figure 1-4. The Project 2003 screen.

You might find the Project 2003 program screen a bit confusing and overwhelming the first time you see it. What are all of those buttons, icons, menus, and lines for? This lesson will help you become familiar with the Project program screen. There are no step-by-step instructions in this lesson—all you have to do is look at Figure 1-4 to see what everything you're looking at means. Relax! This lesson is only meant to help you get acquainted with the Project screen. You don't have to memorize anything.

1 Open Microsoft Project 2003.

The default view, Gantt Chart view, appears on your screen as shown in Figure 1-4.

The default screen for Project is the Gantt Chart view, named after Henry Gantt, a consulting engineer from the early 1900s. Gantt wrote a revolutionary paper that claimed workers were human beings, not machines, and should be led, not driven.

2 Find the screen elements listed in Table 1-4.

Familiarize yourself with the parts of the Project 2003 screen.

Table 1-4. The Project 2003 Screen

Element	Description
Bar chart	Displays task information in a bar chart format.
Entry bar	Enter or edit contents of a selected cell in a table.
Menu bar	Displays a list of menus used to give commands to Project. Clicking on a menu name displays a list of commands. For example, clicking the Format menu would display different formatting commands.

Table 1-4. The Project 2003 Screen (Continued)

Element	Description
Scroll bars	There are both vertical and horizontal scroll bars—you use them to view and move around your project. The scroll box shows where you are in the view. For example, if the scroll box is located near the right end of the horizontal scroll bar, you're at the end of the project.
Status bar	Displays the status of certain keys on the keyboard, as well as information about the current command or operation.
Task Entry table	Displays the tasks you enter for your project. Different views display variations of Task Entry tables, and some views don't have a Task Entry table.
Timescale	Displays time in different formats across the tops of some chart views.
Title bar	Shows the name of the file you're using. The Title bar appears at the top of all windows.
Standard toolbar	Toolbars are shortcuts—they contain buttons for the most common commands (instead of wading through several menus). The Standard toolbar contains buttons for the Project commands you use most frequently, such as saving, opening, and printing documents.
Formatting toolbar	Contains buttons for the most common formatting commands, such as applying bold or italic to text.
ID number column	Displays the ID number of a task or resource, depending on the current view.
Project Guide toolbar	Guides you through the correct procedures for building and maintaining a project.

Don't worry if you find some of these objects confusing at first—they will make more sense after you've actually used them.

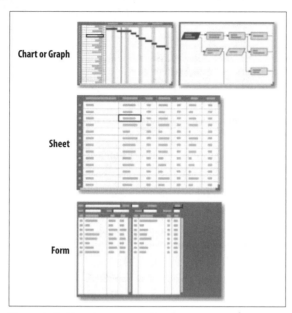

Figure 1-5. Three basic types of views.

Just as there are several different types of database objects in Microsoft Project, there are also many different program screens or views, which makes Project quite different from most Microsoft programs.

The default view for Project is the Gantt Chart view, which is the view you will probably use most often. However, there are many other views in Project. These views allow you to view and work with your project's data more easily. Most of them can be categorized into three basic types of views: chart or graph, sheet, and form (see the illustrations in Figure 1-5).

Each view focuses on information about tasks or resources, depending on what you need to do. This lesson will show you how to switch views, and help you understand the best use for these views.

1 Select View → Task Usage from the menu.

Another way to open a view is to press Alt + V and press the underlined letter in the view name, or click the view button on the View Bar (select View → View Bar from the menu to display the View Bar).

You are now in Task Usage view. This view shows each task and the resources assigned to it, and the cost of each task.

Now try opening Resource Usage view.

2 Select View → Resource Usage from the menu.

Resource Usage view shows each resource, the tasks they are assigned to, and the amount of scheduled work put into each task. You can also view the resources that are overallocated and determine how much time each resource has available for additional work assignments. Let's try viewing a graphic view.

3 Select View → Calendar from the menu.

If you want to see tasks laid out in a month's time, use Calendar view. Calendar view is probably the easiest way to view task schedules, and it is easy to print and hand out to resources so they can see the project schedule without having to learn to use Project.

Now go back to the default view, Gantt Chart.

4 Select View → Gantt Chart from the menu.

But what do all the rest of the views do? To read a description of each common views, refer to Table 1-5.

Table 1-5. Project 2003 Common Views[a]

View	Type	Description
Calendar	Graphic/Task	Displays tasks and durations in a monthly calendar. Use this task view to see tasks scheduled in a specific week or range of weeks.
Gantt Chart	Chart/Task	Displays a list of tasks with bar chart information. Use this task view to enter and schedule tasks.

Table 1-5. Project 2003 Common Views[a] (Continued)

View	Type	Description
Network Diagram	Graphic/Task	Displays a sequence or logic diagram that shows tasks and dependencies. Use this view to create and adjust a schedule in a flow chart format.
Task Usage	Sheet/Task	Displays a list of tasks showing assigned resources under each task. Use this view to see which resources are assigned to which tasks.
Tracking Gantt	Chart/Task	Displays a list of tasks in a table, with a baseline schedule and scheduled Gantt bars for each task. Use this view to compare the baseline and actual schedules.
Resource Graph	Graphic/Resource	Displays a graph showing your resources and their costs, allocations, etc. over time. Use this view to see information about your resources over a specific period of time.
Resource Sheet	Sheet/Resource	Displays a list of resources and their details in rows and columns. Use this view to enter and edit general information for each resource.
Resource Usage	Sheet/Resource	Displays assigned tasks grouped under each resource. Use this view to show work or cost information for each resource.

a. Microsoft Project 2002 Help files, © 1999, Microsoft Corporation.

QUICK REFERENCE

TO CHANGE VIEWS:

* CLICK THE VIEW MENU AND SELECT A NEW VIEW.
  OR...

* PRESS ALT + V AND PRESS THE UNDERLINED
  LETTER IN THE VIEW NAME.

TO DISPLAY THE VIEW BAR:

* SELECT VIEW → VIEW BAR FROM THE MENU.

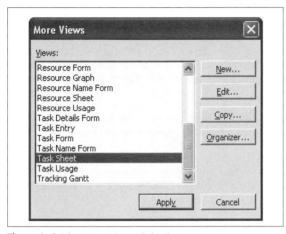

Figure 1-6. The More Views dialog box.

Most of the time, you will be able to see the information you need in one of the common views. When you need to be more specific about the information you view, however, try using one of the views available in the More Views dialog box.

1 Select View → More Views from the menu.

The More Views dialog box appears with more views to choose from, as shown in Figure 1-6.

2 Scroll down the list, select Task Sheet, and click Apply.

The project is shown in Task Sheet view, which is basically a full view of the left half of Gantt Chart view.

3 Select View → Gantt Chart from the menu.

Refer to Table 1-6 for a description of the other views in the More Views dialog box.

Table 1-6. More Views[a]

View	Type	Description and Use
Bar Rollup	Chart/Task	A list of summary tasks and their subtasks. Use this view with the Rollup_Formatting macro to see all tasks concisely labeled on summary task bars.
Descriptive Network Diagram	Graphic/Task	This view is basically the same as Network Diagram view, except the boxes are larger, which allows you to display more information about tasks.
Detail Gantt	Chart/Task	A list of tasks and related information, and a chart showing slack and slippage. Use this task view to check how far a task can slip without affecting other tasks.
Leveling Gantt	Chart/Task	A list of tasks, information about task delays and slack, and a bar chart showing the before and after effects of leveling. Use this task view to check the amount of task delay.
Milestone Date Rollup	Chart/Task	A list of summary tasks containing labels for all subtasks. Use this view with the Rollup_Formatting macro to see all tasks concisely labeled with milestone marks and dates on summary task bars.
Milestone Rollup	Chart/Task	A list of summary tasks containing labels for all subtasks. Use this view with the Rollup_Formatting macro to see all tasks concisely labeled with milestone marks on summary task bars.
Multiple Baselines Gantt	Chart/Task	A Gantt Chart showing the first three baselines saved for the project, each in a different color.

Table 1-6. More Views[a] (Continued)

View	Type	Description and Use
Relationship Diagram	Graphic/Task	A network diagram showing the predecessors and successors of one task. In a large project, use this task view to focus on the task dependencies of a specific task.
Resource Allocation	Sheet & Chart/Resource	A combination view, with the Resource Usage view in the top pane and the Leveling Gantt view in the bottom pane. Use this resource view to resolve resource overallocations.
Resource Form	Form/Resource	A form for entering and editing information about a specific resource.
Resource Name Form	Form/Resource	A form for entering and editing the resource name and other resource information.
Task Details Form	Form/Task	A form for reviewing and editing detailed tracking and scheduling information about a specific task.
Task Entry	Graphic & Form/Task	A combination view, with the Gantt Chart view in the top pane and the Task Form view in the bottom pane. Use this task view to add, edit, and review detailed information about the task.
Task Form	Form/Task	A form for entering and editing information about a specific task.
Task Name Form	Form/Task	A form for entering and editing the task name and other task information.
Task Sheet	Sheet/Task	A list of tasks and related information. Use this task view to enter and schedule tasks in a spreadsheet-like format.

a. Microsoft Project 2002 Help files, © 1999, Microsoft Corporation.

QUICK REFERENCE

TO USE MORE VIEWS:

1. SELECT VIEW → MORE VIEWS FROM THE MENU.

2. SELECT A VIEW IN THE DIALOG BOX.

3. CLICK APPLY.

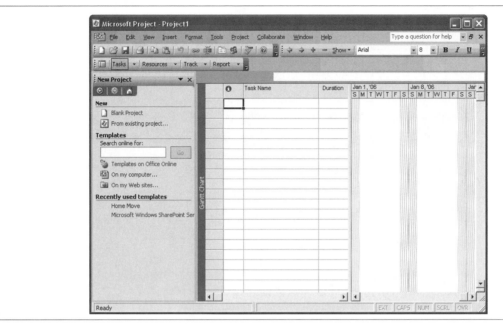

Figure 1-7. The New Project task pane.

Once you have your project all planned out, you can begin entering it in a new file. Project automatically opens to a new file, but you don't have to re-open the program every time you want to start a new file. This lesson shows you all you need to know about opening a new file.

For now, concentrate on creating a new Blank Project file.

1 Select File → New from the menu.

Another way to open a new project file is to click the ☐ New button on the Standard toolbar, or press Ctrl + N.

The New Project task pane appears, as shown in Figure 1-7. Here you can open a blank project, choose a project template, or open an existing project.

2 Click the Blank Project link in the New Project task pane.

The new Project file appears on the screen, along with the Project Guide. If you want, just follow along with the instructions to begin creating the project.

Table 1-7 is a suggestion of steps to take when starting a new project file. Not all of them are necessary, depending on the size and scope of your project. Don't worry if you don't know how to do some of these things; just keep following along in the book, and you'll learn eventually.

⸱ NOTE ⸱ *The Project Guide is a useful resource to use when creating your project. Follow its steps to set up and create your project.*

Table 1-7. Starting a Project File

Step	Description
Create a Project file	The first step in creating your project is to open the file you will use throughout your project. You can start a new file, or you can base your new file on an existing file or template.
Enter the Project Scheduling Date	Enter the start or finish date of the project. It's easiest to schedule tasks from the start date.
Enter project properties	**Optional:** File properties, such as the project title or the company name, can help you and others in the organization identify and locate your file in the future.
Link or store project-related documents in Project	**Optional:** After you have created a file, attach your project's planning-related documents to it so they are easy to access.
Select the Project Calendar	The Project Calendar defines the working time for tasks and resources in the project.
Set the working time for the Project Calendar	You may need to change the working days and hours for your Project Calendar. In Microsoft Project, the default working time is Monday through Friday, 8:00 a.m. to 12:00 p.m. and 1:00 p.m. to 5:00 p.m. (allotting an hour for lunch). You can change working hours for all working days, specific days (such as every Thursday), or certain dates such as holidays or vacation days.

One of the more difficult aspects of Project is understanding the terminology of all the items in the program. Refer to Table 1-8 for a brief list of common terms that will help you understand the different parts of a project.

Table 1-8. Project Terms and Definitions

Term	Definition
Task	An activity that has a beginning and an end. Projects are made up of tasks.
Resource	The people, equipment, and material used to complete tasks in a project.
Working Time	Hours designated in a Resource or Project Calendar during which work can occur.
Calendar	The scheduling mechanism that determines working time for resources and tasks. The three calendars you will probably work with most often are: **Project Calendar:** Schedules the default working hours for the project. **Resource Calendar:** Use if the resource requires working hours that are different from the Project Calendar. **Task Calendar:** Use if the task requires working hours that are different from the Project Calendar. Use the available base calendars as templates for the calendars you use in your project.
Baseline	A snapshot of the project schedule at the time you save the baseline.

Table 1-8. Project Terms and Definitions (Continued)

Term	Definition
Cost	The total cost for a task, resource, or assignment. A baseline cost is referred to as the project's budget.
Report	A format in which you can print the status of the project that is appropriate for the intended audience.
Assignment	A specific resource assigned to a specific task.

QUICK REFERENCE

TO CREATE A NEW PROJECT:

1. SELECT FILE → NEW FROM THE MENU.

2. CLICK BLANK PROJECT IN THE TASK PANE.

   OR...

• CLICK THE NEW BUTTON.

   OR...

• PRESS CTRL + N.

The project will be scheduled from the Start date, so the Finish date is shaded.

Figure 1-8. The Project Information dialog box.

After creating a new project file, entering basic project information—like the project's start date—is the first step. Enter as much information as you know about the project in this dialog box before entering any tasks. It doesn't take long to fill out, but the information is important because it affects how Project goes about scheduling your project.

1 Select Project → Project Information **from the menu.**

The Project Information dialog box appears, as shown in Figure 1-8.

The most important piece of information to enter is the start or end date. First, you have to decide if you want to plan your project from the start date, or the end date.

- **Start Date:** If you plan it from the start date, Project will assign the tasks to begin As Soon As Possible (ASAP), so the project doesn't have to be drawn out longer than necessary.

- **Finish Date:** If you plan it from the finish date, Project will assign the tasks to begin As Late As Possible (ALAP) so the project will be completed on the appointed date.

2 Click the Schedule from **list arrow. Select the scheduling option you want to use.**

"Project Start Date" is the default setting of Project Information, and is the most common way to schedule a project.

Now, enter the project's start or finish date, depending on how you chose to schedule the project.

3 Enter the project's Start date or Finish date.

One of these options will be grayed out, depending on how you chose to schedule the project, as shown in Figure 1-8.

Finally, select the calendar for the project. Go on to the next lesson to learn more about setting up your Project Calendar.

> **QUICK REFERENCE**
>
> **TO ENTER THE SCHEDULING DATE:**
>
> 1. SELECT PROJECT → PROJECT INFORMATION FROM THE MENU.
>
> 2. CLICK THE SCHEDULE FROM LIST ARROW AND SELECT A SCHEDULING OPTION.
>
> 3. ENTER THE PROJECT'S START DATE OR FINISH DATE.

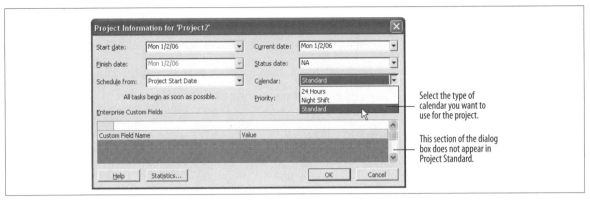

Figure 1-9. The Project Information dialog box.

The Project Calendar is a schedule of working hours for all the tasks and resources in your project. The default Standard calendar schedules a work week from 8 a.m. to 5 p.m. on Monday through Friday, but there are two other calendars you can choose from if your project doesn't fit this schedule.

This lesson will show you how to choose a calendar that's right for your project.

1 If necessary, select Project → Project Information from the menu.

The Project Information dialog box appears, as shown in Figure 1-9.

There are three types of calendars you can choose from:

- **Standard:** Standard work day and work week of Monday through Friday, 8:00 a.m. to 5:00 p.m., with a 12:00 p.m. to 1:00 p.m. lunch break. The Standard option is the default option, and the most common calendar option.
- **24 Hours:** Working time is scheduled nonstop from Sunday through Saturday, 12:00 a.m. to 12:00 p.m.
- **Night Shift:** Working time is scheduled Monday night through Saturday morning, 11:00 p.m. to 8:00 a.m., with 3:00 a.m. to 4:00 a.m. for a non-working lunch break.

Now, select the calendar that best matches a typical work schedule for the project.

2 Click the Calendar list arrow and select the calendar you want to use. Click OK.

 Your Project Calendar should reflect typical working time for the project. You can make changes to calendars for specific resources and tasks as necessary.

Once you choose the calendar, you can further modify it to fit your needs. Go on to the next lesson to learn how.

QUICK REFERENCE

TO SET THE PROJECT CALENDAR:

1. SELECT PROJECT → PROJECT INFORMATION FROM THE MENU.

2. CLICK THE CALENDAR LIST ARROW AND SELECT THE CALENDAR YOU WANT TO USE.

3. CLICK OK.

Adjusting Working Hours

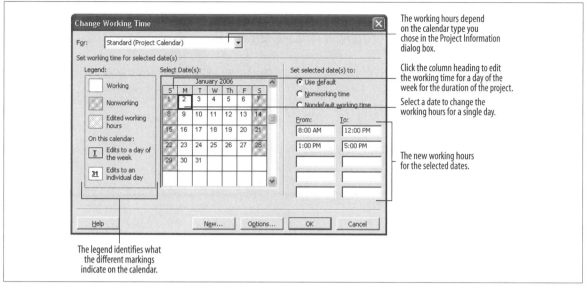

The working hours depend on the calendar type you chose in the Project Information dialog box.

Click the column heading to edit the working time for a day of the week for the duration of the project.

Select a date to change the working hours for a single day.

The new working hours for the selected dates.

The legend identifies what the different markings indicate on the calendar.

Figure 1-10. The Change Working Time dialog box

If your Project Calendar working hours don't quite fit the typical hours at your company, you can easily modify them. For example, if your business opens later in the day, you can change the week's working hours to be from 10 a.m. to 7 p.m. You can also change the working hours for a single day of the week if, for example, you close early on Saturdays. This lesson will show you how to change the working hours for your Project Calendar.

1 Select Tools → Change Working Time **from the menu.**

The Change Working Time dialog box appears, as shown in Figure 1-10.

2 Select the date(s) you want to change in the Select Date(s) section.

You can change the working hours for a single day or a day of the week. Or you can use the Shift and Ctrl keys to select multiple dates and change them all at the same time.

TIP

To select multiple dates or days of the week, press the Shift key to select adjacent dates or column headings. Press the Ctrl key to select nonadjacent dates or column headings.

In our example, we selected the column headings for Monday through Friday to change the working time for all days of the work week.

3 Enter the new working hours in the To: and From: text boxes.

The working hours for the selected dates are changed, and the affected dates are shaded to indicate edited working hours.

Notice that you can break up working hours into several segments if necessary.

4 Click OK.

Q: What's the difference between changing a date and a day of the week?

A: When you change the working hours for a day of the week, that day is changed for the duration of the project. For example, selecting the Saturday column heading will modify the working hours for all Saturdays in the project. However, changing the hours for a date affects only that day. For example, selecting December 31, New Year's Eve, and changing the hours to close down the office early will affect only that day.

QUICK REFERENCE

TO CHANGE WORKING HOURS:

1. SELECT *TOOLS* → *CHANGE WORKING TIME* FROM THE MENU.

2. SELECT THE DATE(S) YOU WANT TO CHANGE.

   DAY OF THE WEEK: CLICK THE COLUMN HEADING(S) OF THE DAYS YOU WANT TO CHANGE FOR THE DURATION OF THE PROJECT.

   DATE: SELECT THE DATE(S) YOU WANT TO CHANGE.

3. ENTER THE NEW WORKING HOURS IN THE *TO:* AND *FROM:* TEXT BOXES.

4. CLICK *OK*.

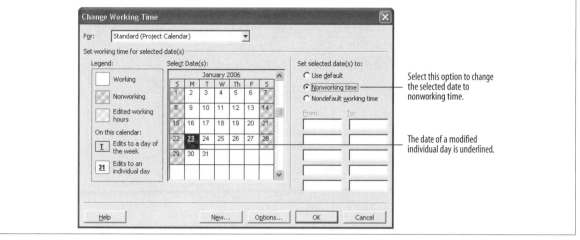

Figure 1-11. The Change Working Time dialog box.

In addition to changing working hours, you can also modify the working days for the entire project. For example, you can schedule days when no work will be done on the project as nonworking days, such as holidays. This lesson will show you how to add nonworking days to your Project Calendar.

1 Select Tools → Change Working Time from the menu.

The Change Working Time dialog box appears.

There are a number of reasons to schedule nonworking days: holidays, days when you know resources will be devoted to other projects, etc.

2 Select the date(s) you want to change in the Select Date(s) section.

You can select a single date (or dates) to make it a nonworking day, like the Fourth of July. You can also change the working time for a day of the week. For example, if people are scheduled to work four 10-hour days Monday through Thursday, you would schedule Friday as a nonworking day every week.

3 Click the Nonworking time option in the dialog box.

Notice that there are no working hours scheduled in the From: and To: columns of the dialog box, as shown in Figure 1-11.

4 Click OK.

Changing a day to a nonworking day is not permanent. You can always add hours to a nonworking day to make it a working day again.

QUICK REFERENCE

TO SCHEDULE NONWORKING TIME:

1. SELECT TOOLS → CHANGE WORKING TIME FROM THE MENU.

2. SELECT THE DATE(S) YOU WANT TO CHANGE.

   DAY OF THE WEEK: CLICK THE COLUMN HEADING(S) OF THE DAYS YOU WANT TO CHANGE FOR THE DURATION OF THE PROJECT.

   DATE: SELECT THE DATE(S) YOU WANT TO CHANGE.

3. CLICK THE NONWORKING TIME OPTION IN THE DIALOG BOX.

4. CLICK OK.

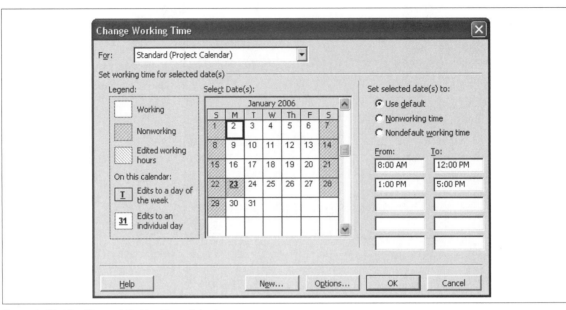

Figure 1-12. The Change Working Time dialog box.

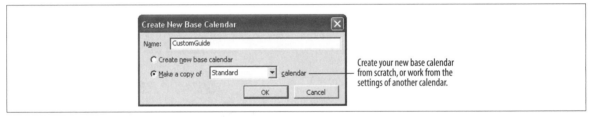

Figure 1-13. The Create New Base Calendar dialog box.

There are three types of base calendars in Project: Standard, 24 Hours, and Night Shift. You can use these calendars to schedule working hours for the project and individual tasks and resources. But sometimes none of these base calendars quite fit the schedule, and you will have to create your own base calendar. Here's how…

1 Select Tools → Change Working Time from the menu.

The Change Working Time dialog box appears, as shown in Figure 1-12.

2 Click the New button in the dialog box.

The Create New Base Calendar dialog box appears, as shown in Figure 1-13.

3 Type the calendar name in the Name text box.

When you want to assign the new calendar to the task, this is the name you will look for.

Notice that there are two options to choose from in the dialog box:

• **Create a new base calendar:** Select this option if you want to create an entirely new calendar.

• **Make a copy of:** Instead of creating an entirely new calendar, copy an existing base calendar and change the working time to make a new calendar.

4 Click the calendar option you want to use. Select the base calendar you want to copy, if necessary.

If you choose to make a copy, your calendar will be based on the schedule for that calendar.

5 Click OK.

The Change Working Time dialog box appears once again, but this time you are going to change the working time for the new calendar.

6 Change the working hours and nonworking days for the new calendar as necessary in the Change Working Time dialog box.

Once you've made the necessary changes, you're ready to finish creating your new base calendar.

7 Click OK.

The dialog box closes and the new base calendar is saved in your project. Now you can assign your new calendar to any resource, or even use it as your Project Calendar if you want.

QUICK REFERENCE

TO CREATE A NEW BASE CALENDAR:

1. SELECT TOOLS → CHANGE WORKING TIME FROM THE MENU.

2. CLICK THE NEW BUTTON IN THE DIALOG BOX.

3. ENTER THE CALENDAR NAME IN THE NAME TEXT BOX.

4. CLICK THE CALENDAR OPTION YOU WANT TO USE AND CHOOSE THE BASE CALENDAR YOU WANT TO COPY, IF NECESSARY.

5. CLICK OK.

6. CHANGE THE WORKING HOURS AND NONWORKING DAYS FOR THE CALENDAR AS NECESSARY.

7. CLICK OK.

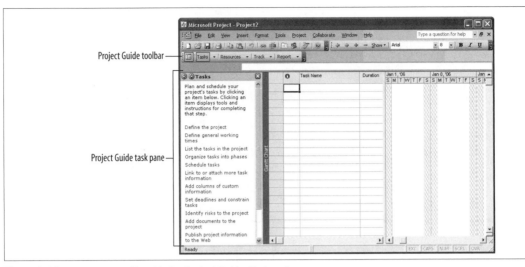

Project Guide toolbar —

Project Guide task pane —

Figure 1-14. A new project file with the Project Guide displayed.

A new feature introduced in Project 2002, and probably the most helpful feature for beginners, is the Project Guide (as shown in Figure 1-14). The Project Guide is like an advanced wizard that guides you through each step in creating a project: entering tasks and resources, recording progress, reporting project status, and so on. The Project Guide appears whenever you create a new project file, but you can turn the Project Guide off once you are more familiar with how to build a project.

There are two ways to use the Project Guide:

- **Project Guide toolbar:** This toolbar provides access to instructions and wizards in each of four basic project elements: Tasks, Resources, Track, and Report.

- **Project Guide task pane:** The task pane contains a list of tasks for each basic project element, and provides the necessary instructions and wizards to help you accomplish those tasks.

In this lesson, we will explore the Project Guide.

1 If you can't see the Project Guide task pane, click the  Show/Hide Project Guide button on the Project Guide toolbar.

TIP *To view or hide the Project Guide toolbar, select* View → Toolbars → Project Guide *from the menu.*

The Project Guide task pane displays the steps for working with tasks.

Let's try a step in the Tasks category.

2 Click the Define general working times link in the Project Guide task pane.

The first step in defining the project's working times appears.

Notice that there are two arrows at the top of the guide, which you can use to progress between steps in the wizard. If you were actually creating a project, you would just follow the arrows.

If you know the exact step you want help with, you can quickly access it from the Project Guide toolbar.

3 Click the Resources button list arrow on the Project Guide toolbar.

A list of all the steps available in the Resources category of the Project Guide appears.

4 Select Specify people and equipment for the project from the list.

The options for entering resources appear in the task pane. Also, notice that the view changes from Gantt Chart to Simple Resource Sheet. The Project Guide recognizes the action being performed—in this case, entering resources—and changes the view to accommodate the steps.

If the task pane is taking up too much room, you can close it and work only from the Project Guide toolbar.

5 Click the Show/Hide Project Guide button on the Project Guide toolbar.

 TIP *To turn off the Project Guide, select* Tools → Options *from the menu, click the* Interface *tab, and uncheck the* Display Project Guide *checkbox.*

The task pane disappears.

One of the great advantages of the Project Guide is that even if you know how to create a project, you can still use the Project Guide to view the different methods or options available to perform a step. Refer to Table 1-9 for a listing of the steps that the Project Guide covers.

Table 1-9. Project Guide Steps

Tasks	
Define the project	Link to or attach more task information
Define general working times	Add columns of custom information
List the tasks in the project	Set deadlines and constrain tasks
Organize tasks into phases	Add documents to the project
Schedule tasks	Publish project information to the Web

Resources	
Specify people and equipment for the project	Link to or attach more resource information
Define working times for resources	Add columns of custom information
Assign people and equipment to tasks	Publish project information to the Web

Track	
Save a baseline plan to compare with later versions	Prepare to track the progress of your project
Incorporate progress information into the project	Check the progress of the project
Make changes to the project	Track issues associated with this project
Request text-based status reports	Publish project information to the Web

Report	
Select a view or report	Change the content or order of information in a view
Change the look or content of the Gantt Chart	Print current view as a report (new feature in Project 2003)
Compare progress against baseline work	See the project's critical tasks
See how resources' time is allocated	See project costs

QUICK REFERENCE

TO VIEW THE PROJECT GUIDE TOOLBAR:

- SELECT VIEW → TOOLBARS → PROJECT GUIDE FROM THE MENU.

TO USE THE PROJECT GUIDE:

1. ON THE PROJECT GUIDE TOOLBAR, CLICK THE CATEGORY BUTTON YOU WANT TO WORK ON.

2. CLICK THE LINK TO THE STEP YOU WANT TO COMPLETE IN THE PROJECT.

3. FOLLOW THE PROJECT GUIDE'S INSTRUCTIONS TO COMPLETE THE SETUP.

OR...

CLICK ANY BUTTON LIST ARROW ON THE PROJECT GUIDE TOOLBAR AND SELECT THE STEP YOU WANT TO COMPLETE.

TO TURN OFF THE PROJECT GUIDE:

- SELECT TOOLS → OPTIONS FROM THE MENU. CLICK THE INTERFACE TAB AND UNCHECK THE DISPLAY PROJECT GUIDE CHECKBOX.

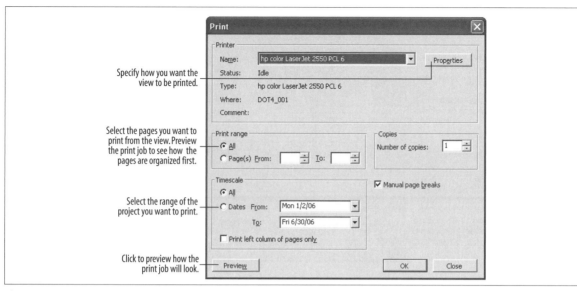

Specify how you want the view to be printed.

Select the pages you want to print from the view. Preview the print job to see how the pages are organized first.

Select the range of the project you want to print.

Click to preview how the print job will look.

Figure 1-15. The Print dialog box.

When you want to print exactly what's on your screen, print a view. Total graphical information will print in all printable views. However, in views that contain tables, only the visible table columns will print along with the graphical information. You can print any view, except for form views and the Relationship Diagram view.

Before you print a project view, you should complete any formatting you want to appear on your view, use the spellchecker, insert page breaks, and preview the view.

1 Open the view you want to print.

In this case, we are going to print the Gantt Chart, so you don't have to open a different view.

 It's a good idea to preview your project before printing. Select File → Print Preview to open print preview. When you're finished, click Close.

2 Select File → Print from the menu.

The Print dialog box appears.

3 Choose your print options.

You can select which printer to print from, how many copies you want to print, which pages you want to print, and what dates of your project you want to print. Also, you can click the Properties button to choose advanced printing options. Figure 1-15

displays more information on how to specify different options when you print.

4 When you are ready to print, click OK.

The project view prints.

⌇ NOTE ⌇ *For multiple page views (which have page breaks), all of the lefthand pages will print before the righthand pages.*

QUICK REFERENCE

TO PRINT A VIEW:

1. OPEN THE VIEW YOU WANT TO PRINT.

2. SELECT FILE → PRINT FROM THE MENU.

3. CHOOSE YOUR PRINT OPTIONS.

4. WHEN YOU ARE READY TO PRINT, CLICK OK.

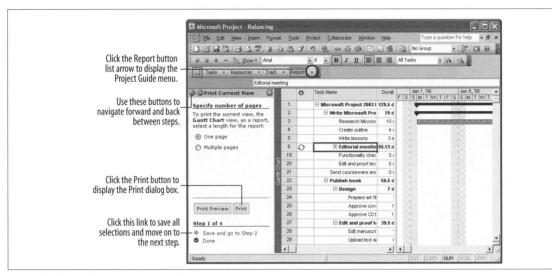

Click the Report button list arrow to display the Project Guide menu.

Use these buttons to navigate forward and back between steps.

Click the Print button to display the Print dialog box.

Click this link to save all selections and move on to the next step.

Figure 1-16. The first step in printing the current view as a report.

If you thought printing a view was easy, wait until you try printing the current view as a report. Making its debut in Project 2003, the "Print current view as a report" option is one of the best things to come along since sliced bread! Well, maybe not, but it is definitely worth checking out.

Located in the Report task pane of the Project Guide, the "Print current view as a report" option acts as a wizard, guiding you through each and every step of printing the current view as a report. Let's get acquainted with this brand-new option!

1 Open the view you want to print.

In this case, we'll be using Gantt Chart view, so you don't have to open a new view.

2 Click the Report list arrow on the Project Guide toolbar and select Print current view as a report from the list.

To view or hide the Project Guide toolbar, select View → Toolbars → Project Guide from the menu.

The first step of the wizard in the Print Current View task pane appears, as shown in Figure 1-16. Navigate through each step by clicking the link at the bottom of the task pane.

3 Click the Save and go to Step 2 link at the bottom of the task pane.

Step 2 of the wizard appears. Go ahead and work your way through the next two steps in the wizard, familiarizing yourself with the various options offered.

4 Click the Print button when you've finished working through all four steps.

The Print dialog box appears. You can also click the Print Preview button to see how the report will be printed.

We aren't going to be printing anything in this lesson, so...

5 Close the dialog box and the Project Guide task pane.

QUICK REFERENCE

TO PRINT THE CURRENT VIEW AS A REPORT:

1. OPEN THE VIEW YOU WANT TO PRINT.

2. CLICK THE REPORT LIST ARROW ON THE PROJECT GUIDE TOOLBAR AND SELECT PRINT CURRENT VIEW AS A REPORT FROM THE LIST.

3. WORK YOUR WAY THROUGH THE WIZARD.

4. CLICK THE PRINT BUTTON IN THE TASK PANE WHEN YOU'RE FINISHED.

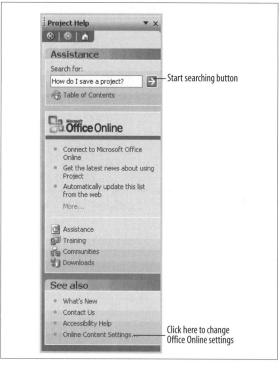

Start searching button

Click here to change
Office Online settings

Figure 1-17. Asking a question in the Project Help task pane.

Click the Search list
arrow to select Offline
Help.

Figure 1-18. Search for Offline Help results.

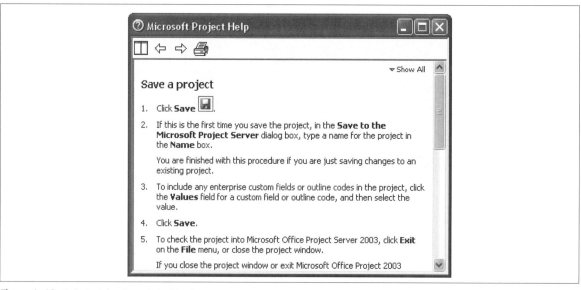

Figure 1-19. Help text for the selected topic.

When you don't know how to do something in Windows or a Windows-based program, don't panic, just look up your question in the Project Help files. The Project Help files can answer your questions, offer tips, and provide help for all of Project's features. Many Project users forget to use Help, and this is unfortunate because the Help files know more about Project than most reference books do!

You can make the Project Help files appear by pressing the F1 key. Then, all you have to do is ask your question. This lesson will show how you can get help by asking the Help files a question about a specific Project feature.

1 Press the F1 key.

Another way to get help is to type your question in the Type a question for help box on the menu bar and press Enter. The results appear in the Project Help task pane. You can also get help by clicking the Table of Contents link in the Project Help task pane and searching by topic.

The Project Help task pane appears, as shown in Figure 1-17.

2 Type How do I save a project? in the Search for: text box, as shown in Figure 1-17.

You can ask Project Help questions in normal English, just as if you were asking a person instead of a computer. The program identifies keywords and phrases in your questions, such as "save" and "project."

⋮ NOTE ⋮ *Microsoft has totally changed the way Help works in Office 2003 with Office Online. Instead of searching for help in the files already stored on your computer, Office Online searches for the topic in its online database. The purpose of this feature is to provide current, up to date information on search topics.*

3 Click the Start searching button.

Office Online will refer to Offline Help files if a connection to the Internet is not detected.

Office Online finds results like "Save a project to work on offline" and "Troubleshoot saving projects."

Fortunately, you can change your settings to perform Help searches without Office Online. Go to the "See also" section at the bottom of the Project Help task pane. Click the Online Content Settings link, uncheck the Search online content when connected option, and click OK.

4 Click the Search list arrow in the Search section at the bottom of the task pane. Select Offline Help from the list, as shown in Figure 1-18. Click the Start searching button.

The Offline Help search results appear in the task pane.

5 Click the Save a project help topic.

Project displays information on how to save a project, as shown in Figure 1-19.

Notice that the Microsoft Office Project Help window has a toolbar that looks like some of the buttons you might have seen on a web browser. This lets you navigate through each help topic just as if you were browsing the Web. See Table 1-10 to find out what each of these buttons mean.

6 Click the Microsoft Office Project Help window's Close button to close the window.

The Help window closes.

Table 1-10. Help Buttons

Button	Description
⇦	Moves back to the previous help topic.
⇨	Moves forward to the next help topic.
🖶	Prints the current help topic.
⊟	Tiles the Project program window and the Help window so you can see both at the same time.

QUICK REFERENCE

TO GET HELP:

1. PRESS THE F1 KEY.

2. TYPE YOUR QUESTION IN THE SEARCH FOR: TEXT BOX AND CLICK THE START SEARCHING BUTTON OR PRESS ENTER.

3. CLICK THE HELP TOPIC THAT BEST MATCHES WHAT YOU'RE LOOKING FOR (REPEAT THIS STEP AS NECESSARY).

TO TURN OFF OFFICE ONLINE:

1. CLICK THE ONLINE CONTENT SETTINGS LINK IN THE PROJECT HELP TASK PANE.

2. UNCHECK THE SEARCH ONLINE CONTENT WHEN CONNECTED OPTION AND CLICK OK.

Chapter One Review

Lesson Summary

Planning the Project

Before entering information in a project file, you must have a clear idea of the scope and purpose of the project.

Understanding Project Management

A Project is a temporary series of actions undertaken to create a unique product or service.

All Projects:

• have a start and end date
• are efforts made by people or equipment
• create a product or service

The Project Triangle Includes: Time, Cost, and Scope.

Understanding the Project Screen

Be able to identify the main components of the Project program screen.

Using Common Views

To Change Views: Select the View menu and select a new view. Or, press Alt + V and press the underlined letter in the view name.

To Display the View Bar: Select View → View Bar from the menu.

Using More Views

To Use More Views: Select View → More Views from the menu. Select a view in the dialog box and click Apply.

Creating a New Project

To Create a New Project: Select File → New from the menu and click Blank Project in the task pane. Or click the New button, or press Ctrl + N.

Entering the Project Scheduling Date

To Enter the Scheduling Date: Select Project → Project Information from the menu. Click the Schedule from list

arrow and select a scheduling option. Enter the project's Start date or Finish date.

Selecting the Project Calendar

To Set the Project Calendar: Select Project → Project Information from the menu. Click the Calendar list arrow and select the calendar you want to use. Click OK.

Adjusting Working Hours

To Change Working Hours: Select Tools → Change Working Time from the menu. Select the date(s) you want to change:

• **Day of the Week:** Click the column heading(s) of the days you want to change for the duration of the project.
• **Date:** Select the date(s) you want to change. Enter the new working hours in the To and From text boxes.

Click OK.

Adjusting Working Days

To Change Nonworking Time: Select Tools → Change Working Time from the menu. Select the date(s) you want to change:

• **Day of the Week:** Click the column heading(s) of the days you want to change for the duration of the project.
• **Date:** Select the date(s) you want to change.

Click the Nonworking time option in the dialog box and click OK.

Creating a New Base Calendar

To Create a New Base Calendar: Select Tools → Change Working Time from the menu. Click the New button in the dialog box and enter the calendar name in the Name text box. Click the calendar option you want to use, and choose the base calendar you want to copy, if necessary. Click OK. Change the working hours and nonworking days for the calendar as necessary and click OK.

Using the Project Guide

To View the Project Guide Toolbar: Select View → Toolbars → Project Guide from the menu.

To Use the Project Guide: On the Project Guide toolbar, click the category button you want to work on. Click the link to the step you want to complete in the project and follow the Project Guide's instructions to set up the project. Or, click any button list arrow on the Project Guide toolbar and select the step you want to complete.

To Turn Off the Project Guide: Select Tools → Options from the menu. Click the Interface tab and uncheck the Display Project Guide checkbox.

Printing the Project

To Print a Project: Select File → Print from the menu. Choose your print options. When you are ready to print, click OK.

Printing the Current View as a Report

To Print the Current View as a Report: Open the view you want to print. Click the Report button list arrow on the Project Guide toolbar and select Print current view as a report from the list. Work your way through the steps of the wizard and click the Print button when finished.

Getting Help

To Get Help: Press the F1 key, type your question in the Search for: text box, and click the Start searching button or press Enter. Click the help topic that best matches what you're looking for (repeat this step as necessary).

To Turn Off Office Online: Click the Online Content Settings link in the Project Help task pane. Uncheck the Search online content when connected option and click OK.

Quiz

1. What is NOT a component of the project triangle?
   A. Effort
   B. Time
   C. Scope
   D. Cost

2. The default view for Project 2003 is:
   A. Resource Sheet view
   B. Inter view
   C. Gantt Chart view
   D. There is no default view for Project 2003

3. Changes to working hours and nonworking days in the Project Calendar affect the working time of everyone on your project. (True or False?)

4. Which of these is NOT a way to open a new project file?
   A. Select File → New from the menu.
   B. Press the New button.
   C. Press Ctrl + N.
   D. Select Insert → New Task from the menu.

5. How can you access Microsoft Help? (Select all that apply.)
   A. Press F1.
   B. Select Help → Contents and Index from the menu.
   C. Press the Help button.
   D. Click your heels and chant "Microsoft Help, Microsoft Help, Microsoft Help" three times.

6. You can change views in Project 2003 by (select all that apply):

   A. selecting a new view from the View Bar (if it is displayed).

   B. hiding your toolbars.

   C. going to the View menu and selecting a new view.

   D. pressing Alt + V and pressing the underlined letter in a new view.

7. Most databases have the ability to share information. (True or False?)

8. Which of the following is NOT a category in the Project Guide?

   A. Reports

   B. Track

   C. Tasks

   D. Collaboration

9. Creating a new base calendar affects the Project Calendar. (True or False?)

Homework

1. Start Microsoft Project 2003.

2. Navigate to your practice files and open the Homework 1 project.

3. Switch to Resource Sheet view and then back to Gantt Chart view.

4. Select the first task, "Open a Lemonade Stand," and change it to "Open a Slim-Fast Stand."

5. Change the Project Calendar to Night Shift.

6. Add a nonworking day for December 25.

7. Close the Homework 1 database.

Quiz Answers

1. A. Effort is not a component of the project triangle.

2. C. Gantt Chart view is the default view in Project 2003.

3. True. The Project Calendar is the default calendar used by everyone in the project.

4. D. This procedure will only insert a new task in the task list.

5. A and C. Pressing F1 and clicking the Help button will access Microsoft Help.

6. A, C, and D. You cannot change views by hiding your toolbars. If you want to use the View Bar but it does not appear on your screen, select View → View Bar from the menu.

7. True. Most databases can share information; very few cannot.

8. D. Collaboration is not a category covered in the Project Guide.

9. False. Creating a new base calendar simply gives you more calendar options to choose from; it doesn't affect the Project Calendar, unless you choose to use it as such.

CHAPTER 2
ENTERING THE TASK LIST

CHAPTER OBJECTIVES:

Enter tasks and task durations, Lessons 2.1–2.3

Create a milestone, Lesson 2.4

Organize the task list, Lesson 2.5

Link, unlink, and split tasks, Lessons 2.6–2.8

Create a recurring task, Lesson 2.9

Use task information and notes, Lessons 2.10 and 2.11

Add a hyperlink to a task, Lesson 2.12

Learn how to insert, delete, copy, and move tasks, Lessons 2.13 and 2.14

Prerequisites

- **Understand project management.**
- **Know the basic elements of Project 2003.**

Once you have your project file set up (with your start date and project calendar), you can begin putting together your project. This chapter deals with the driving force behind most projects—tasks. In this chapter, we are going to enter and organize a list of tasks to be completed in the project. We'll also begin to estimate the duration of tasks, which will give us an idea of how long the project will take.

Diving into a blank project can be very intimidating. Just thinking of all that needs to be done to complete a project, much less setting it up, can feel completely overwhelming. But as long as you take it step by step, Project will do all the calculating and scheduling for you, making the process much more manageable.

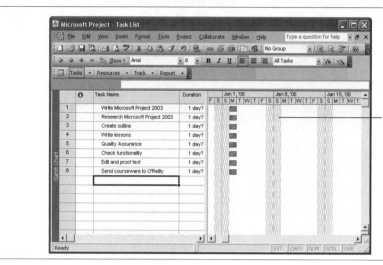

Project enters as much task information as it can, based on the data it already has about the project.

Figure 2-1. Entering tasks in the project.

Tasks are the engines that propel the progress of a project. A task represents an amount of work with a clear outcome. As tasks are worked on, Project calculates their effect on the overall outcome of the project. If you have done a good job of project planning, you should already have an idea of what you need to do to accomplish your project's goals. So crack your knuckles and get ready—it's time to enter tasks into your project!

1 Navigate to your Practice folder and open the Lesson 2 file. Save the file as Task List.

2 Click the first cell of the Task Name field.

When entering a task, pick a name that clearly identifies the purpose of the task.

3 Type Write Microsoft Project 2003 and press Enter.

The task is named and numbered.

Enter a few more tasks into the project.

4 Repeat Step 3 to enter the following tasks:

Research Microsoft Project 2003
Create outline
Write lessons
Quality Assurance
Check functionality
Edit and proof text
Send courseware to O'Reilly

Your task list should look similar to Figure 2-1. Notice that even though you haven't entered anything more than the task name, Project has entered more information for the task based on the information it already has about the project.

QUICK REFERENCE

TO ENTER A TASK:

• TYPE THE TASK'S NAME IN THE TASK NAME FIELD, AND PRESS ENTER.

Estimating Task Duration

Duration abbreviations used in Microsoft Project

Abbreviation	How it appears in Project	What it means
m	min	minute
h	hr	hour
d	day	day
w	wk	week
mo	mon	month

Figure 2-2. You can use abbreviations to indicate duration length in Project.

Once you've entered tasks in the project, you need to tell the program how long each task will take. Project then uses the durations you enter to calculate the amount of time the project will take as a whole.

How does Project calculate how long the task will take? First, Project looks at the amount of active working time you have available from the start to the end of the task. Then, Project looks at the amount of working time you estimate that the task will take to complete, which is the amount of time you enter in the Duration field.

For example, the Standard calendar is dedicated to 40 hours of work on the project each week. Therefore, Project assumes that one day requires eight hours, one week requires 40 hours, etc. When you estimate that a task will take two weeks to finish, Project assumes that you need 80 hours to do it.

Here are some guidelines to help you estimate a task's duration:

- **Consider the scope of the project:** Durations can be entered in months, weeks, days, hours, or minutes. It all depends on the scope of the entire project. For example, if you are trying to plan a project that will take several years to complete, it is probably useless to plan the duration of a task in minutes.

- **Refer to the entire project:** Generally, if you have a longer project, you will have longer tasks, and if you have a shorter project, you will have shorter tasks.

Sound confusing? You'll understand better as you continue to work with more of the features in Project.

There is another type of duration you can use in a project—elapsed durations. Elapsed durations ignore working and nonworking time in all calendars and resource assignments. They schedule tasks 24 hours a day, seven days a week, until they are finished. Elapsed durations are useful for processes that can't stop once started, such as the period of time it takes cement to cure after it is poured. You designate an elapsed duration by entering an "e" before the duration unit—for example, "4 ed" for four elapsed days. Figure 2-2 describes the various abbreviations used to indicate duration length in Project.

QUICK REFERENCE

- ESTIMATING THE DURATION OF A TASK IS PROBABLY THE HARDEST PART OF ENTERING TASKS. TO DO A GOOD JOB OF ESTIMATING THE DURATION OF A TASK, RESEARCH THE TASKS OF SIMILAR PROJECTS THAT HAVE ALREADY BEEN COMPLETED.

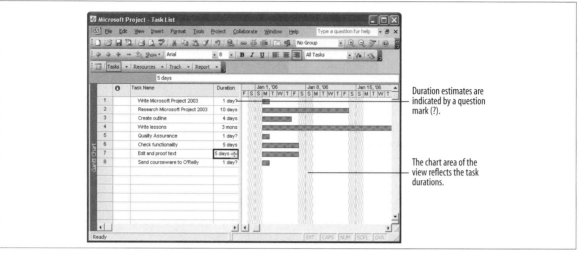

Figure 2-3. The project updated with task durations in Gantt Chart view.

Now that you know the basics of task duration, it's time to get to work.

1 Click the Duration field for the "Research Microsoft Project 2003" task.

Notice that there is already a value entered in the field. The question mark indicates that the number is an estimate, which is what Project automatically enters in the task field until you assign a more definite duration.

Give yourself ten days to research the program.

2 Type 10 days and press Enter.

The insertion point moves down to the next task duration and the chart area changes to reflect the task's duration.

⋮ NOTE ⋮ *We entered 10 days for the duration of this task, but because 1 week = 5 days, Project calculates 10 days and two weeks as having the same number of working hours.*

3 Enter the following durations for their corresponding tasks:

Task Number	Task Name	Duration
3	Create outline	4 days
4	Write lessons	3 months

Task Number	Task Name	Duration
5	Quality Assurance	(skip for now)
6	Check functionality	5 days
7	Edit and proof text	5 days
8	Send courseware to O'Reilly	(skip for now)

The Gantt Chart updates to show the duration of the tasks, as shown in Figure 2-3.

QUICK REFERENCE

TO ENTER A DURATION:

• ENTER A DURATION IN THE DURATION FIELD.

Entering a Milestone

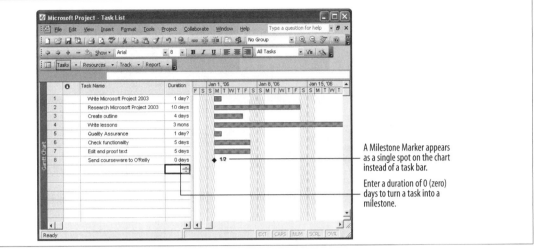

Figure 2-4. A milestone in the project.

Your project will be full of tasks that need to be completed by the time you're done with it, but it's also important to track events that occur in your project. In this example, finishing the book and sending it to the publisher is a big deal. Such events are *milestones*, tasks that mark significant events in your project. Milestones can also be used to mark a deadline or some other type of restriction imposed on the project.

Though milestones don't require any work, they are useful additions to the project.

1 **Click the Duration field for the "Send courseware to O'Reilly" task.**

This task is a significant marking point in the project.

There are two ways to change a task into a milestone: enter a duration of 0 (zero) days in the duration field, or mark the task as a milestone in the Task Information dialog box.

2 **Type 0 days and press Enter.**

The "Send courseware to O'Reilly" task has been changed into a milestone, as shown in Figure 2-4.

The milestone in this example is ideal, because sending something at its completion is an indicator of progress, but it doesn't really take much time to do.

Milestones are very easy to use. Don't be afraid to use them as markers for the beginning or ending of a task. You might even want to use them as reference points—for example, to mark the halfway point of a project's progress.

QUICK REFERENCE

TO CREATE A MILESTONE:

- ENTER A DURATION OF 0 (ZERO) DAYS FOR A TASK.

  OR...

- CLICK THE TASK INFORMATION BUTTON AND CLICK THE ADVANCED TAB, CHECK THE MARK TASK AS MILESTONE CHECKBOX, AND CLICK OK.

Organizing Tasks into Phases

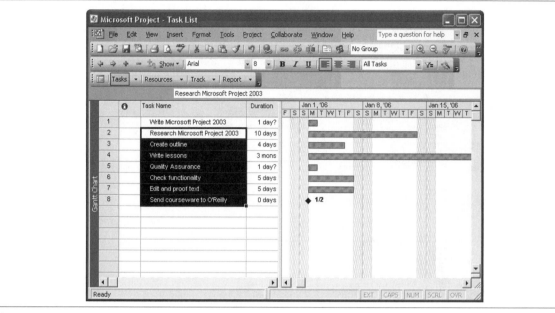

Figure 2-5. Selecting subtasks in the list.

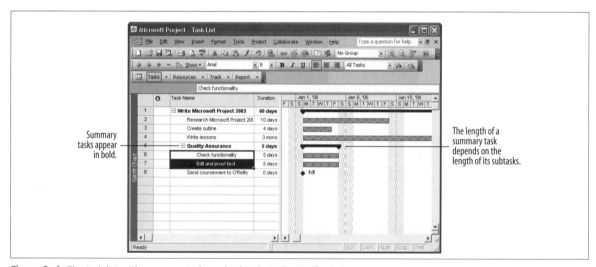

Figure 2-6. The task list with summary tasks and subtasks in Gantt Chart view.

The more tasks you have in a project, the more confusing things can become. Therefore, it's helpful to organize your tasks into phases, or groups of related tasks. In Project, phases are grouped by *summary tasks*. Tasks underneath the summary tasks are called *subtasks*. By organizing the tasks into phases, it's easier to tell how the tasks are related to each other.

Project calculates the duration of a summary task by the duration of its subtasks. So if you change information in your subtasks, the duration of your summary task will change.

1 Click the Research Microsoft Project 2003 task. Then, press and hold down the Shift key and select the Send courseware to O'Reilly task.

The tasks are selected, as shown in Figure 2-5. These tasks will be subtasks of the summary task, "Write Microsoft Project 2003."

⸱ NOTE ⸱ *You can also click and drag to select multiple tasks at a time.*

A summary task is created when its subtasks are indented below it.

2 Click the  Indent button on the Formatting toolbar.

Task 1, "Write Microsoft Project 2003," becomes a summary task, and tasks 2 through 8 become subtasks.

⸱ NOTE ⸱ *The level of a task's indentation tells you whether it's a summary task or a subtask.*

You can also nest summary tasks within summary tasks.

3 Select the Check functionality task. Then, press and hold down the Shift key and select the Edit and proof text task. Click the Indent button on the Formatting toolbar.

Tasks 6 and 7 become subtasks of the Quality Assurance summary task. Your task list should look similar to Figure 2-6.

Notice that the summary task bars appear in black and extend as far as the longest subtask.

Organizing your tasks into phases is pretty intuitive. If you want to hide the subtasks under a summary task, click the collapse button next to the summary task or click the Hide Subtasks button on the Formatting toolbar. If you want to view the subtasks again, click the expand button next to the summary task, or click the Show Subtasks button on the Formatting toolbar.

QUICK REFERENCE

TO CREATE A SUMMARY TASK:

1. UNDER THE SUMMARY TASK, SELECT THE TASKS YOU WANT TO USE AS SUBTASKS.

2. CLICK THE INDENT BUTTON ON THE FORMATTING TOOLBAR.

TO VIEW THE SUBTASKS OF A SUMMARY TASK:

• CLICK THE SHOW SUBTASKS BUTTON ON THE FORMATTING TOOLBAR.

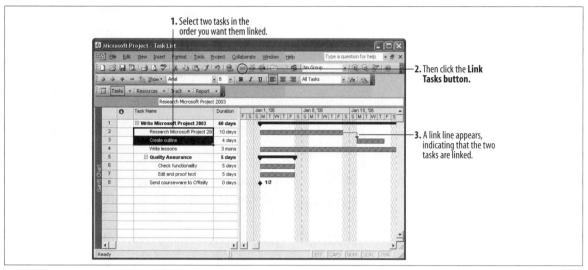

Figure 2-7. The process for linking tasks.

Scheduling tasks is another very important part of the project. It's impossible to predict the start or finish date for every task in the project, but it is possible to know how the tasks' schedules are related. For instance, you can't write a book about anything until you have researched it. Likewise, you can't send a book to a publisher until you've finished writing it. By linking these tasks, Project knows that a task relationship has been created and that their schedules are dependent upon one another.

A task dependency is the relationship between two tasks, in which the start or finish date of one task depends on the start or finish date of another. The task whose start or finish date depends on another task is called the *successor*. The task that the successor is dependent upon is the *predecessor*. The most common task dependency is a finish-to-start dependency. In this type of dependency, the second task in the relationship starts when the first task is finished. For example, when the "Create outline" task is finished, the "Write lessons" task can start. Let's try it…

1 Select the Research Microsoft Project 2003 **task.**

You must select tasks in the order that you want them linked. This task will be the predecessor in the relationship.

2 Press and hold the Shift **key and select the** Create outline **task.**

To select nonadjacent tasks, hold down the Ctrl *key and click the task name. To select adjacent tasks, hold down the* Shift *key and click the first and last task you want to link.*

The two selected tasks are ready to be linked.

3 Click the Link Tasks button **on the Standard toolbar.**

Another way to link tasks is to select Edit → Link Tasks *from the menu, or press* Ctrl + F2, *or click and drag the predecessor task bar to the successor task bar in the Gantt chart.*

The two tasks are now linked by a link line, as shown in Figure 2-7. Notice that the bar for the "Create outline" task moves to the end of the "Research Microsoft Project 2003" task. This indicates that the "Create outline" task will start when the "Research Microsoft Project 2003" task is finished.

You can also click and drag to select adjacent tasks.

4 Click the Create outline **task and drag to select the** Write lessons **task. Click the** Link Tasks button **on the Standard toolbar.**

Another task relationship is created.

You should always try to link tasks of the same type, even if they are subtasks of different summary tasks. For example, you shouldn't link a subtask to a summary task. To link nonadjacent tasks, use the Ctrl key.

5 Select the Write lessons **task. Press and hold the** Ctrl **key and select the** Check functionality **task.**

Remember that the summary task's schedule depends on its subtasks, so the schedule for the "Quality Assurance" task will also change if the "Check functionality" task's schedule changes.

6 Click the Link Tasks button **on the Standard toolbar.**

The selected tasks are linked.

If you want to create the same type of relationship between a number of tasks, you can link several tasks at once.

7 Select the Check functionality **task. Press and hold the** Shift **key and select the** Send courseware to O'Reilly **task. Click the** Link Tasks **button on the Standard toolbar.**

The selected tasks are all linked to one another.

8 Select the Check functionality **task and click the** Go To Selected Task button **on the Standard toolbar.**

Project jumps to the selected task in the Gantt chart and shows how the tasks are linked in the project.

QUICK REFERENCE

TO LINK TASKS:

1. PRESS SHIFT TO SELECT ADJACENT TASKS.

   OR...

   PRESS CTRL TO SELECT NONADJACENT TASKS.

(NOTE: SELECT TASKS IN THE ORDER BY WHICH YOU WANT THEM TO BE DEPENDENT.)

2. CLICK THE LINK TASKS BUTTON.

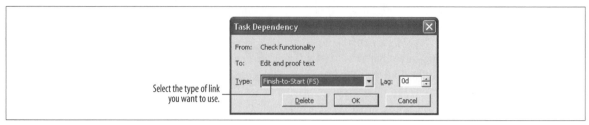

Figure 2-8. The Task Dependency dialog box.

By default, a Finish-to-Start dependency is created when tasks are linked. But there are other types of task dependencies Project can use. For example, tasks can be linked by a Start-to-Start dependency, which means they begin at the same time. Here's how to change the type of link between tasks.

1 Select the Check functionality **task and click the** Go To Selected Task **button on the Standard toolbar.**

The Gantt chart shows the relationship between the "Check functionality" and "Edit and proof text" tasks. The "Edit and proof text" task can really be done at the same time as the "Check functionality" task, so change the link type.

2 **Double-click the** link line **between the "Check functionality" and "Edit and proof text" tasks.**

The Task Dependency dialog box appears, as shown in Figure 2-8.

Notice that the dialog box displays which tasks the link is from and to.

3 **Click the** Type **list arrow and select the** Start-to-Start (SS) **option. Click** OK.

Notice that the schedule of the "Edit and proof text" task changes so that it will start on the same day as the "Check functionality" task. Check out Table 2-1 for information on other links you can use in your project.

Table 2-1. Types of Links

Link Type	Description	Looks Like...
Finish-to-Start (FS)	The successor task will begin when the predecessor task ends. This is the default type of link.	
Start-to-Start (SS)	Both the predecessor and successor tasks begin at the same time. The start date of the predecessor task determines the start date for the successor task.	
Finish-to-Finish (FF)	Both the predecessor and successor tasks end at the same time. The end date of the predecessor task determines the end date for the successor task.	
Start-to-Finish (SF)	The successor task will end when the predecessor task begins. Use this link to minimize the risk of a task finishing late, such as for a milestone or a project end date.	

QUICK REFERENCE

TO EDIT A TASK LINK:

1. DOUBLE-CLICK THE LINK LINE BETWEEN THE LINKED TASKS.

2. CLICK THE TYPE LIST ARROW AND SELECT THE TYPE OF LINK YOU WANT TO USE.

3. CLICK OK.

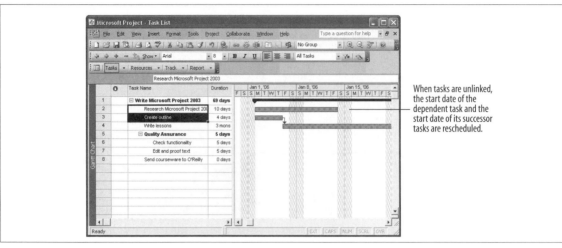

When tasks are unlinked, the start date of the dependent task and the start date of its successor tasks are rescheduled.

Figure 2-9. Unlinking task dependencies.

Fortunately, links between tasks are not permanent. You may need to remove a link because of scheduling changes or create a dependency with a different task. But be aware that once a task link is broken, its schedule and the schedules of its successors are changed.

Here's how to unlink tasks.

1 Select the Research Microsoft Project 2003 task, and then press the Shift key and select the Create Outline task.

Once the linked tasks are selected, they are ready to be unlinked.

2 Click the Unlink Tasks button.

Another way to unlink tasks is to select Edit → Unlink Tasks *from the menu.*

The two tasks are unlinked, and the start date of the "Create outline" task is rescheduled to the project start date, as shown in Figure 2-9.

Notice that all of its successor tasks are also affected by the change. When unlinking tasks in your project, always make sure to create another task relationship for the unlinked tasks. This will put your project schedule back on track.

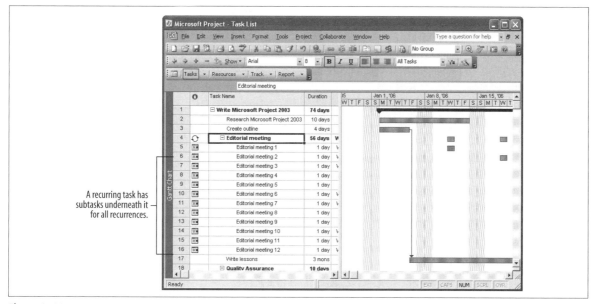

Figure 2-10. The Recurring Task Information dialog box.

Figure 2-11. A recurring task and its subtasks.

Recurring tasks are tasks that repeat regularly. A recurring task can take place daily, weekly, monthly, or yearly. You can specify how long the repeating tasks will take, when the tasks will occur, and how long the recurrence pattern should continue.

Let's create a recurring task for weekly editorial meetings.

1 Select the Write lessons task. Select Insert → Recurring Task from the menu.

The Recurring Task Information dialog box appears, as shown in Figure 2-10.

First, name the task.

2 Type Editorial meeting in the Task Name box.

Now enter the duration of the recurring task.

3 Type 2 hours **in the** Duration **box.**

Now specify how often you want the task to recur.

4 **Select the** Weekly **option and click the** Wednesday **checkbox for the day of the week.**

This recurring task will occur every week on Wednesday.

Now, define when the recurring tasks should begin and how long they will last. The recurrence pattern can end after a specific number of times, or the pattern can continue until a certain date. You can enter your own "end by" date; otherwise, Project enters the project's current latest date.

In this example, the recurring task should start and finish with the "Write lessons" task. This "end by" date is already entered in the dialog box, so you don't have to make any changes here.

5 **Click the** Start **list arrow and select** January 6, 2006 **from the calendar menu.**

This is the date that the "Write lessons" task is scheduled to begin.

6 **Click the** End by **option. Click the** End by **list arrow and select** March 30, 2006 **from the calendar menu.**

Now the editorial meetings will recur for the duration of the "Write lessons" task.

⋮ NOTE ⋮ *You cannot create links to task relationships, so knowing the start and end dates of the recurrence is very important.*

Compare your dialog box to Figure 2-10.

7 **Click** OK **to close the Recurring Task Information dialog box.**

The Recurring Task Information dialog box closes.

Notice that the new task is entered and that there is an expand button (⊞) next to its task name.

8 **Click the** expand button (⊞) **in the Editorial meeting task.**

All the recurrences of the task appear, as shown in Figure 2-11.

9 **Click the** collapse button (⊟) **in the Editorial meeting task.**

The recurring tasks are hidden once again.

Once recurring tasks are created, you can reschedule all the tasks at once by changing the original recurring task, or you can change individual recurring tasks without affecting the other subtasks.

QUICK REFERENCE

TO CREATE A RECURRING TASK:

1. SELECT INSERT → RECURRING TASK FROM THE MENU.

2. ENTER THE RECURRING PATTERN INFORMATION INTO THE RECURRING TASK INFORMATION DIALOG BOX AND CLICK OK.

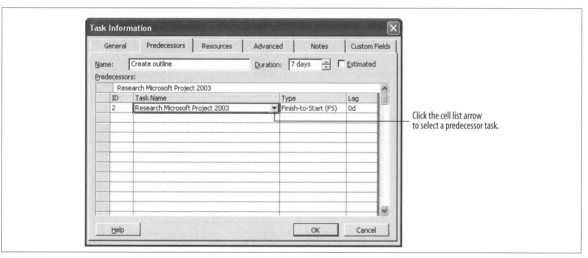

Figure 2-12. The General tab of the Task Information dialog box.

Click the cell list arrow
to select a predecessor task.

Figure 2-13. The Predecessors tab of the Task Information dialog box.

So far, you have been working with tasks in the default Gantt Chart view, but you can also work with many task properties in the Task Information dialog box.

This lesson contains an overview of the ways you can use the Task Information dialog box when you're working with tasks.

1 Select the Create outline task and click the Task Information button on the Standard toolbar. Click the General tab.

> **TIP**
> Another way to open the Task Information dialog box is to right-click the task and select Task Information from the shortcut menu, or select the task and press Shift + F2.

The Task Information dialog box appears, as shown in Figure 2-12.

One property you can change is the duration of a task.

2 Click the Duration text box and type 7 days.

Terrific! You have just changed a task's information.

Notice that in this tab you can also change the name of a task and the task's start or finish date, and you can even track the progress of the task in the "Percent complete" box.

3 Click the Predecessors tab.

The task's predecessors appear, as shown in Figure 2-13. You can add or change links to the current task here.

4 Click the first empty cell in the Task Name column.

You can link tasks by selecting a predecessor task.

5 Click the cell list arrow and select the Research Microsoft Project 2003 task. Press Enter.

> **TIP**
> To edit multiple tasks at a time, select the group of tasks you want to edit and click the Task Information button. Make edits in the Multiple Task Information dialog box. Do this only if you are sure the tasks will have the same information.

A Finish-to-Start relationship has been created, with the "Research Microsoft Project 2003" task as the predecessor.

The information in the General and Predecessors tabs should be familiar, but there are four other tabs that will be covered later in this book. Table 2-2 briefly describes each tab in the Task Information dialog box.

Table 2-2. Task Information dialog box

Tab	Description
General	Use this tab to enter, review, or change basic information about the selected task. For example, change task durations, track task progress, and enter a start or finish date.
Predecessors	Use this tab to enter, review, or change predecessor information about the selected task. Enter a predecessor for the current task and select the predecessor type, and enter lag time or lead time.
Resources	Use this tab to enter, review, or change resource assignments and assignment units for the selected task.
Advanced	Use this tab to enter, review, or change supplemental task information. For example, enter a deadline for the task, change a task constraint, specify the task calendar, or mark the task as effort-driven or as a milestone.
Notes	Use this tab to enter or review notes for a selected task. For example, add new notes about a task, revise existing notes, format the font and alignment of notes, or insert objects into a note.
Custom Fields	Use this dialog box to view and assign values to task custom fields and outline codes.

QUICK REFERENCE

TO OPEN THE TASK INFORMATION DIALOG BOX:

- CLICK THE TASK INFORMATION BUTTON ON THE STANDARD TOOLBAR.

  OR...

- RIGHT-CLICK THE TASK AND SELECT TASK INFORMATION FROM THE SHORTCUT MENU.

  OR...

- SELECT THE TASK AND PRESS SHIFT + F2.

Figure 2-14. The Notes tab of the Task Information dialog box.

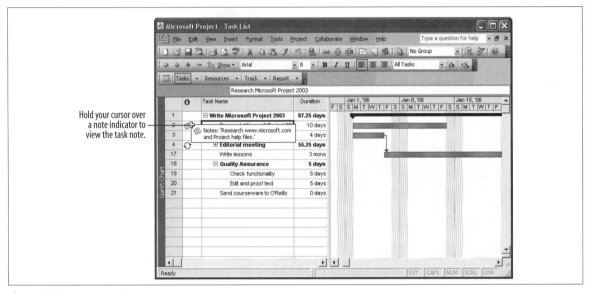

Hold your cursor over a note indicator to view the task note.

Figure 2-15. Viewing task notes.

Task notes are a valuable way to add detailed descriptions about what needs to be done in a task. A task's notes are easily viewed by everyone in the project, so as project manager you don't have to repeat the same information.

1 Click the Research Microsoft Project 2003 task. Click the 📝 Task Notes button on the Standard toolbar.

The Task Information dialog box appears with the Notes tab in front, as shown in Figure 2-14.

Let's enter some information on how to go about researching Microsoft Project.

2 Type Research www.microsoft.com and Project help files, and click OK.

The Task Information dialog box closes. Notice that a little yellow note icon now appears next to the task. The fastest way to view a task note is to hold your cursor over it until its screen tip pops up.

3 Hold your cursor over the 📝 note indicator of the "Research Microsoft Project 2003" task.

A screen tip of the task note appears, as shown in Figure 2-15. If the note is too long, double-click the indicator to view the entire note.

QUICK REFERENCE

TO ENTER A TASK NOTE:

- CLICK THE TASK NOTES BUTTON ON THE STANDARD TOOLBAR.

    OR...

- RIGHT-CLICK THE TASK AND SELECT TASK NOTES FROM THE SHORTCUT MENU.

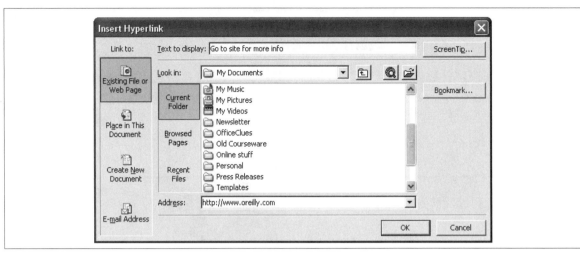

Figure 2-16. The Insert Hyperlink dialog box.

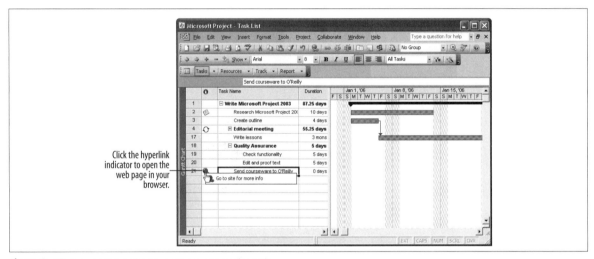

Click the hyperlink
indicator to open the
web page in your
browser.

Figure 2-17. A hyperlink indicator appears next to the task.

Task notes can manage most of the details you will want to add to a task. However, if you want to add information from an online source, such as a web page, you can place a hyperlink right next to the task.

1 Select the Send courseware to O'Reilly task.

Let's add a link to the O'Reilly web site for this task.

2 Click the  Insert Hyperlink button on the Standard toolbar.

The Insert Hyperlink dialog box appears, as shown in Figure 2-16.

Enter descriptive text for the link and the address of the page you want to link to.

3 Type Go to site for more info in the Text to display: text box.

This text will appear as the screen tip.

4 Type http://www.oreilly.com in the Address: text box. Click OK.

The Insert Hyperlink dialog box closes. Notice that a hyperlink indicator now appears next to the task. Hold your cursor over the indicator to view the descriptive text you entered (as shown in Figure 2-17), or click the indicator to open the web page in your browser.

QUICK REFERENCE

TO INSERT A HYPERLINK:

1. CLICK THE INSERT HYPERLINK BUTTON ON THE STANDARD TOOLBAR.

   OR...

   RIGHT-CLICK THE TASK AND SELECT HYPERLINK FROM THE SHORTCUT MENU.

2. ENTER DESCRIPTIVE TEXT IN THE TEXT TO DISPLAY TEXT BOX.

3. ENTER THE WEB ADDRESS IN THE ADDRESS TEXT BOX.

4. CLICK OK.

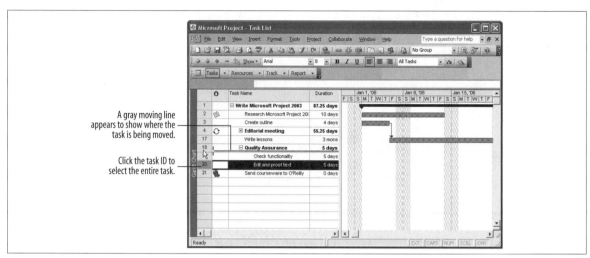

A gray moving line appears to show where the task is being moved.

Click the task ID to select the entire task.

Figure 2-18. Moving a task in Gantt Chart view.

As you work with entering tasks in your project, you will find that you need to reorder some of them. This lesson covers how to move and copy tasks, commands you may find useful when working with tasks in your project.

⁞ NOTE ⁞ *It is best not to move or copy tasks that are linked. This will affect the links and relationships that have been created.*

1 Click the task ID of the task you want to move.

Once the task is selected, you can move it to a new location in the list. To rearrange the order of tasks, it's easiest to move them by clicking and dragging.

2 Click and drag the task to the end of the list.

A gray line indicates where the task is being moved, as shown in Figure 2-18.

You can also copy tasks in the project.

3 Click the task ID of the task you want to copy.

Once the task is selected, you can copy it.

4 Select Edit → Copy Task from the menu.

The task has been copied and placed on the clipboard. Now let's insert the copied task.

5 Click the task ID where you want to paste the copied task.

The copied task will be inserted above the selected task.

6 Select Edit → Paste from the menu.

The copied task is pasted above the selected task.

QUICK REFERENCE

TO MOVE A TASK:

1. SELECT THE TASK ID.

2. CLICK AND DRAG THE TASK TO A NEW LOCATION IN THE TASK LIST.

TO COPY A TASK:

1. CLICK THE TASK ID OF THE TASK YOU WANT TO COPY.

2. SELECT EDIT → COPY TASK FROM THE MENU

   OR...

RIGHT-CLICK THE SELECTED TASK AND SELECT COPY TASK FROM THE SHORTCUT MENU.

OR...

SELECT THE TASK AND PRESS CTRL + C.

TO PASTE A COPIED TASK:

1. CLICK THE TASK ID OF THE TASK YOU WANT THE COPIED TASK TO APPEAR ABOVE.

2. SELECT EDIT → PASTE FROM THE MENU.

Inserting and Deleting a Task

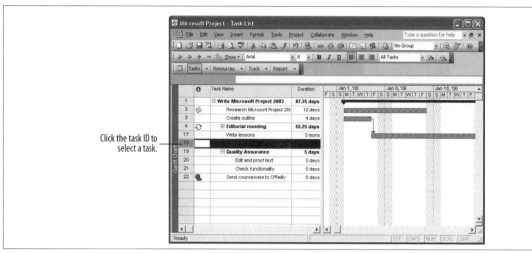

Figure 2-19. Working with tasks in the project.

Click the task ID to select a task.

This lesson will show you how to insert new tasks and delete tasks you no longer need.

First, let's insert a new task in the project.

1 **Click the task ID where you want to insert the new task.**

The new task will be inserted above the selected task.

2 **Select Insert → New Task from the menu.**

A new task is entered into the project, as shown in Figure 2-19.

If you find that you don't need a task in the project, you should delete it. However, deleting tasks could decrease the overall quality of the project, so make sure the task you are planning to remove does not affect any other tasks.

3 **Click the task ID of the task you want to delete.**

Make sure you click the task ID—this selects the entire task, not just the contents of a cell. For example, simply clicking the task name and pressing Delete will clear the *name* of the task, but it won't delete the task itself.

4 **Select Edit → Delete Task from the menu.**

The task is deleted from the task list, and the remaining tasks are automatically renumbered.

Chapter Two Review

Lesson Summary

Entering a Task

To Enter a Task: Type the task's name in the Task Name field, and press Enter.

Entering Task Durations

To Enter a Duration: Enter a duration in the Duration field.

Creating a Milestone

To Create a Milestone: Enter a duration of 0 (zero) days for a task. Or, click the Task Information button and select the Advanced tab, check the Mark task as Milestone checkbox, and click OK.

Creating a Summary Task

To Create a Summary Task: Under the summary task, select the tasks you want to use as subtasks. Click the Indent button on the Formatting toolbar.

To View the Subtasks of a Summary Task: Click the Show Subtasks button on the Formatting toolbar.

Linking Tasks

To Link Tasks: Press the Shift key to select adjacent tasks, or press the Ctrl key to select nonadjacent tasks. Make sure to select the tasks in the order you want to link them, and then click the Link Tasks button.

Editing Task Links

To Edit a Task Link: Double-click the link line between the linked tasks. Click the Type list arrow and select the type of link you want to use, and then click OK.

Unlinking Tasks

To Unlink Tasks: Press Ctrl while you select two linked tasks in the order they are linked, and then press the Unlink button on the Standard toolbar.

Creating Recurring Tasks

To Create a Recurring Task: Select Insert → Recurring Task from the menu, enter the recurring pattern information into the Recurring Task Information dialog box, and click OK.

Using the Task Information Dialog Box

To Open the Task Information Dialog Box: Click the Task Information button on the Standard toolbar, or right-click the task and select Task Information from the shortcut menu, or select the task and press Shift + F2.

Using Task Notes

To Enter a Task Note: Select a task and click the Task Notes button on the Standard toolbar, or right-click the task and select Task Notes from the shortcut menu.

Using Task Hyperlinks

To Insert a Hyperlink: Click the Insert Hyperlink button on the Standard toolbar, or right-click the task and select Hyperlink from the shortcut menu. Enter descriptive text in the Text to display: text box and enter the web address in the Address: text box. Click OK when you're finished.

Moving and Copying a Task

To Move a Task: Select the task ID of the task you want to move, and then drag the task to a new location.

To Copy a Task: Select the task ID of the task you want to copy. Select Edit → Copy Task from the menu, or right-click the selected task and select Copy Task from the shortcut menu, or select the task and press Ctrl + C.

To Paste a Copied Task: Click the task ID of the task you want the copied task to appear above and select Edit → Paste from the menu.

Inserting and Deleting Tasks

To Insert a Task: Click the task ID of the task you want your new task to appear above, and then select Insert → New Task from the menu, or right-click the task and select New Task from the shortcut menu, or press the Insert key.

To Delete a Task: Click the task ID of the task you want to delete and select Edit → Delete Task from the menu, or click the task ID and press the Delete key, or right-click the task and select Delete from the shortcut menu.

Quiz

1. When you click a linked task, it jumps to the task to which it is linked. (True or False?)

2. What does the 'w' task duration abbreviation stand for?

   A. worthy of importance

   B. winner

   C. week

   D. winter

3. Which of these is a correct way to delete a task?

   A. Dab white-out on your computer screen over the task.

   B. Right-click the task and select Delete from the menu.

   C. Don't look at the task (out of sight, out of mind).

   D. Paste another task over the one you want to delete.

4. A task that includes several subtasks is called a:

   A. Summary task

   B. Phase Level task

C. Tisk task

D. Microsoft Assistant task

5. A recurring task is a task that repeats irregularly. (True or False?)

6. What is a milestone?

   A. The last task you need to complete for your project to be finished.

   B. A task that signifies a major event in your project.

   C. A task that is behind schedule.

   D. Road markers that Fred, Barney, Betty, and Wilma used.

7. Why would you want to add a hyperlink to a task?

   A. To help you remember to complete the task.

   B. So you can interrupt it and finish it on a later date.

   C. So you can add information about an online source.

   D. To energize your project.

Homework

1. Start Microsoft Project.

2. Navigate to your practice files and open the Homework 2 project.

3. Go to task #23, "Go International," and make it a summary task. The three tasks below it will be its subtasks.

4. Enter a new task above task #12. Name the new task "Make tablecloth from bedsheets."

5. Enter a duration of three days for your new task.

6. Delete task #15, "Dress up in a lemon costume."

7. Insert a recurring task above task #23. Name the task "Mail 'Lemon Leader' newsletter," have it occur monthly on every 1st Friday, and have it start on February 7, 2003, ending after five occurrences.

8. Edit task #20, "Hire a CEO," so that it says, "Hire a rich CEO."

9. Make task #6, "Make a pretty sign," into a milestone.

10. Unlink tasks #3 and #4.

11. Add a note that says "Call Sally for help" to task #5, "Build stand."

12. Close Homework 2 without saving your changes.

Quiz Answers

1. False. In Project 2003, linked tasks are tasks that depend on each other for scheduling reasons.

2. C. The 'w' task duration abbreviation stands for "week."

3. B. To delete a task, right-click the task and select Delete from the menu.

4. A. A Summary task includes several subtasks.

5. False. A recurring task repeats regularly, not irregularly.

6. B. A milestone is a task that signifies a major event towards the completion of your project.

7. C. A hyperlink allows you to add information to a task about an online source, such as a web page.

ENTERING AND ASSIGNING RESOURCES

CHAPTER OBJECTIVES:

Enter People resources, Lesson 3.1

Enter Equipment resources, Lesson 3.2

Enter Material resources, Lesson 3.3

Adjust individual resource working schedules, Lesson 3.4

Use resource notes, Lesson 3.5

Understand effort-driven project scheduling, Lesson 3.6

Assign resources to tasks, Lessons 3.7–3.9

Prerequisites

- **Have a project in which you have already entered tasks.**
- **Understand project management.**

Tasks cannot be completed without *resources*. Resources are the people, equipment, and material needed to complete a project. When you assign a resource to a task, Project 2003 looks at the resource's cost and availability. Cost refers to how much money a resource will require. Availability establishes when a resource can work on a task and for how long. Project does a terrific job of managing the resources assigned to tasks.

Assigning resources to tasks helps to keep things organized in the project. For example, you don't want to accidentally schedule a task to be done when a resource isn't available or forget to find someone to complete a certain task. Setting up resources is especially worthwhile if you have time or money constraints for your project. If you don't enter resource information, Project calculates the time and scope of the project, but you will have no idea how much cost is going into the project.

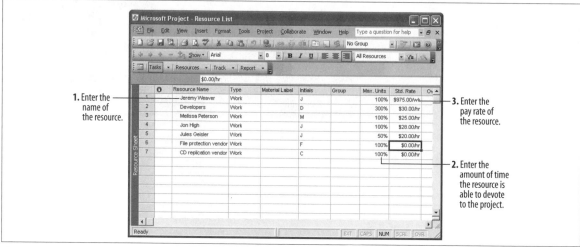

Figure 3-1. Entering people resources in the project.

Once you have created a task list for your project, the next step is to create a resource list. These resources are what allow progress to occur in the project. Project works with two types of resources : work resources and material resources. Work resources are the people and equipment that complete project tasks. Material resources are the goods used by the work resources to complete tasks.

People resources will probably be the most common resources in your project. Let's enter some people resources to do work in the project.

1 Navigate to your Practice folder and open Lesson 3. Save the file as Resource List.

The easiest way to enter resources in a project is to use the Resource Sheet.

2 Select View → Resource Sheet from the menu.

A blank Resource Sheet appears.

3 Click the first cell in the Resource Name field and type Jeremy Weaver. Press Enter.

You can also enter groups of people resources that have common skills. This is especially useful if members of the group do the same thing in the project. For example, a group of three developers do the same thing in the project: create online lessons. While their work is important, it is easier to manage their work as a group (Developers), rather than as individuals.

4 Type Developers and press Enter.

The developers have been added as a resource.

 Individual people resources can be represented by their names (Jeremy Weaver) or job titles (Senior Programmer). Neither way is better than the other, so use names that will make the most sense to the people viewing the project.

5 Repeat Step 4 to enter the following resources:

Melissa Peterson

Jon High

Jules Geisler

File protection vendor

CD replication vendor

The resource names are entered.

 If you do not yet know the name of the resource (for example, if the position or contract has yet to be filled), use a placeholder name.

You should also enter information in the Max. Units and Std. Rate fields.

6 Click the Max. Units field of the Developers resource.

The Max. Units field represents the amount of time the resource will be able to devote to your project. For example, 100% of Jeremy Weaver's time is available to work on tasks assigned to him.

The Developers resource represents three people who are able to spend 100% of their time on assigned tasks, so they have more units.

7 Type 300 in the Developers Max. Units field and press Enter.

Now the project will be able to plan on three developers being available to work full-time on their assigned tasks every day.

The maximum units value for the Jules Geisler resource also needs to change.

8 Type 50 in the Jules Geisler Max. Units field and press Enter.

Project recognizes that Jules is only available to work part-time on the project.

The last bit of information we need is the cost for each resource.

9 Click the Std. Rate field of the Jeremy Weaver resource.

Resources account for a majority of cost in most projects. By tracking this information, the project manager can learn valuable information about expenses in the project, such as whether there will be enough money to cover costs for the duration of the project.

⸱ NOTE ⸱ *You may not be authorized to know the pay rates for resources in your project; that information is usually available only to senior management and human resources. Not having this information will reduce the effectiveness of Project's tracking features, but your supervisors should understand these limitations.*

You can enter rates by hour, day, or week.

10 Type 975/w in the Jeremy Weaver Std. Rate field and press Enter.

Jeremy's standard weekly rate appears in the field.

If a resource represents a number of people, like the Developers and Authors resources, estimate the average rate for each individual.

11 Enter the standard rates for the following resources:

Resource	Std. Rate
Developers	30/h
Melissa Peterson	25/h
Jon High	28/h
Jules Geisler	20/h

Notice that two resources, "File protection vendor" and "CD replication vendor," do not have a standard rate. They are serving as placeholders, because the standard rate won't be known until a vendor has been found for the contract. Compare your list to Figure 3-1.

QUICK REFERENCE

TO OPEN RESOURCE SHEET VIEW:

- SELECT VIEW → RESOURCE SHEET FROM THE MENU.

TO ENTER A PEOPLE RESOURCE:

1. CLICK IN THE RESOURCE NAME FIELD AND ENTER A NAME FOR THE RESOURCE.

2. CLICK IN THE MAX. UNITS FIELD AND ENTER THE RESOURCE'S AVAILABILITY TO THE PROJECT.

3. CLICK IN THE STD. RATE FIELD AND ENTER THE PAY RATE FOR THE RESOURCE.

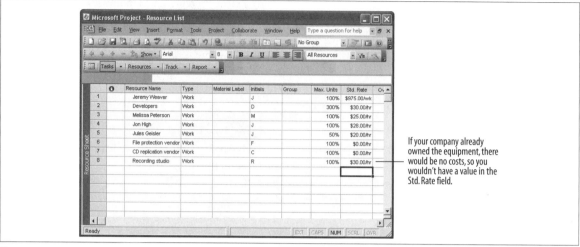

Figure 3-2. Entering an equipment resource in the project.

If your company already owned the equipment, there would be no costs, so you wouldn't have a value in the Std. Rate field.

Equipment resources are also work resources, but they are different from people resources in the way they are used and scheduled. People generally have a set number of working hours that they will contribute to a task each day. But pieces of equipment don't really have a schedule: they can work around the clock if it's needed.

You don't have to track every piece of equipment that is used in the project, but you should keep track of equipment that accumulates cost or that is shared.

Let's enter an equipment resource into the project.

1 Click the empty cell below the CD replication vendor resource in the Resource Name field.

Entering an equipment resource is the same as entering a people resource; both are work resources. The main difference is that equipment has more scheduling flexibility.

2 Type Recording studio and press Tab.

The resource is entered in the list.

3 Click in the Max. Units field of the Recording studio resource.

This field indicates how much time the resource can devote to the project. For example, if you had two recording studios, you could change the data to 200%. Or, if you know the studio is available only part-time because another party is using it, you would enter 50%. For this project, there is one recording studio available all the time, so this data stays at 100%.

4 Click in the Std. Rate field of the Recording studio resource.

The recording studio must be rented by the hour, so we'll enter its hourly rental rate in this field.

5 Type 30 and press Enter.

Compare your project to Figure 3-2.

QUICK REFERENCE

TO ENTER AN EQUIPMENT RESOURCE:

1. CLICK IN THE RESOURCE NAME FIELD AND ENTER A NAME FOR THE RESOURCE.

2. CLICK IN THE MAX. UNITS FIELD AND ENTER THE RESOURCE'S AVAILABILITY TO THE PROJECT.

3. CLICK IN THE STD. RATE FIELD AND ENTER THE COST OF THE RESOURCE.

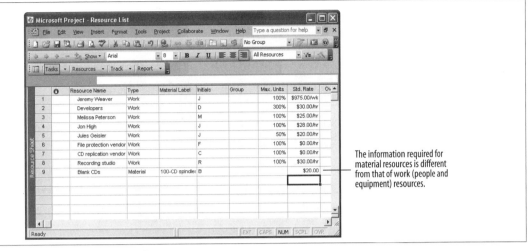

Figure 3-3. Entering a material resource in the project.

Material resources are the goods needed by work resources to complete tasks. Tracking the use of material resources helps track the rate at which the resources are used, as well as their costs. This is especially applicable in building and construction projects that use a lot of materials, such as lumber, steel, or glass.

This project will use a lot of CDs as inserts in the books. Let's enter them as a material resource.

1 Click the empty cell below the Recording studio resource in the Resource Name field. Type Blank CDs and press Tab.

Now define this as a material type of resource.

2 Click the Type field list arrow and select Material from the list. Press Tab.

One field that is important for material resources is the Material Label field. The material label is the unit you use to measure the material resource.

3 Type 100-CD spindles and press Tab.

Project will track the rate and cost of the consumption of 100 CDs at a time.

Next, enter the cost of each spindle of CDs.

4 Click in the Std. Rate field of the Blank CDs resource. Type 20 and press Enter.

Notice that the material's standard rate depends on its consumption; it does not depend on hourly, daily, or

weekly rates. In this case, one spindle of 100 CDs will cost $20 in the project.

Compare your project to Figure 3-3.

QUICK REFERENCE

TO ENTER A MATERIAL RESOURCE:

1. CLICK IN THE RESOURCE NAME FIELD AND ENTER A NAME FOR THE RESOURCE.

2. CLICK THE TYPE FIELD LIST ARROW AND SELECT MATERIAL FROM THE LIST.

3. CLICK IN THE MATERIAL LABEL FIELD AND ENTER THE MATERIAL RESOURCE'S UNIT OF MEASUREMENT.

4. CLICK IN THE STD. RATE FIELD AND ENTER THE RATE FOR THE RESOURCE.

Adjusting Individual Resource Working Schedules

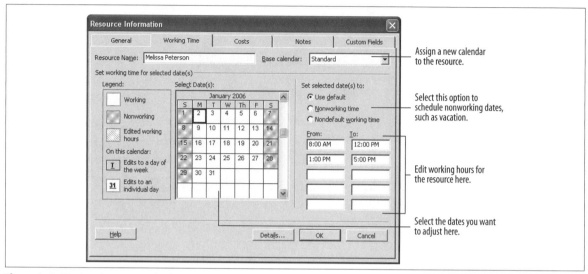

Figure 3-4. The Working Time tab of the Resource Information dialog box.

When you first created your project, you defined a project calendar that would be the default calendar for all the tasks and resources in your project. However, the schedules for resources are still very flexible; you can change an individual resource's working calendar to reflect any time that the resource is not available to work on the project.

For example, if one of the resources works from 10 a.m. to 7 p.m. instead of the default 8 a.m. to 5 p.m., you can adjust that individual's working time without affecting the rest of the project. This is also useful when accounting for vacation or sick days.

Here's how to change working and nonworking times for individual resources.

1 Select the Melissa Peterson resource.

Melissa will be taking a long weekend January 5 and 6 to celebrate her anniversary, so schedule these days as nonworking time.

Now open this resource's calendar.

2 Select Project → Resource Information from the menu.

The Working Time tab of the Resource Information dialog box appears, as shown in Figure 3-4. This dialog

box should be familiar—it's just like the Change Working Time dialog box that controls the calendar for the entire project.

First, find the dates that you want to change.

3 Navigate to the month January 2006 in the Select Date(s) calendar.

Now select the dates you want to change.

4 Click and drag to select the dates January 5 and 6.

Once the dates are selected, you can change the working time or schedule the dates as nonworking time.

5 Click the Nonworking time option in the dialog box. Click OK.

No work will be scheduled for Melissa on these dates.

⋮ NOTE ⋮ *Project Server has a calendar feature that works with Outlook and Project Web access so that resources can automatically report times they are not available to work on a project.*

Now let's look at how to change the working time for a resource.

6 Select the Developers **resource.**

The developers have a different working schedule from the other resources in the project: 10 a.m. to 7 p.m. Change their working times to reflect this.

7 Click the Resource Information button **on the Standard toolbar.**

 Other ways to open the Resource Information dialog box are to select the resource and click the Resource Information button *on the Standard toolbar, or select the resource and press* Shift + F2.

The Working Time tab of the Resource Information dialog box appears.

8 Click the M **column heading and drag to select the** F **column heading.**

The Monday through Friday column headings are selected.

9 Edit the times in the From and To areas of the dialog box to these hours:

From:	To:
10:00 AM	2:00 PM
3:00 PM	7:00 PM

If you must change the working time of several resources, it might be faster to create a new calendar and assign it to the resource.

Project will now know to schedule the developers for work between 10 a.m. and 7 p.m. on working days.

10 Click OK.

The Resource Information dialog box closes.

These schedule changes do not affect the project, because resources have not been assigned to tasks. But keep in mind that once the project is underway, changes like this might affect the scheduling of the project.

QUICK REFERENCE

TO ADJUST AN INDIVIDUAL RESOURCE WORKING SCHEDULE:

1. SELECT THE RESOURCE.

2. SELECT PROJECT → RESOURCE INFORMATION FROM THE MENU.

   OR...

CLICK THE RESOURCE INFORMATION BUTTON ON THE STANDARD TOOLBAR.

OR...

PRESS SHIFT + F2.

3. EDIT THE WORKING TIME FOR THE RESOURCE IN THE DIALOG BOX.

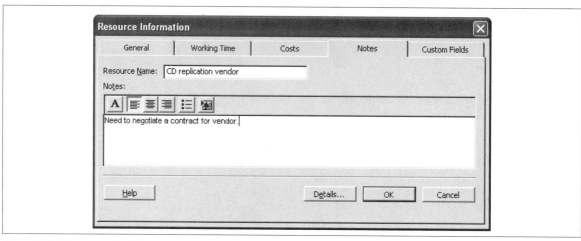

Figure 3-5. The Notes tab of the Resource Information dialog box.

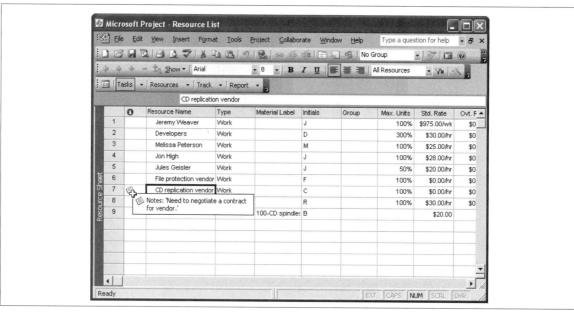

Figure 3-6. Viewing resource notes.

Resource notes are a valuable way to add detailed information about a resource. A resource's notes are easily viewed and are available for everyone in the project, so as project manager you don't have to repeat yourself.

1 Select the CD replication vendor resource. Click the Resource Notes button on the Standard toolbar.

The Resource Information dialog box appears with the Notes tab in front, as shown in Figure 3-5.

Let's add a note that this resource still needs to be secured.

2 Type Need to negotiate a contract for vendor. **Click OK.**

The Resource Information dialog box closes. Notice that a little yellow note icon now appears next to the

resource. The fastest way to view a resource note is to hold your cursor over it to view its screen tip.

3 **Hold your cursor over the**  **note indicator of the CD replication vendor resource.**

A screen tip of the resource note appears, as shown in Figure 3-6. If the note is too long, double-click the indicator to view the entire note.

QUICK REFERENCE

TO ENTER A RESOURCE NOTE:
- CLICK THE RESOURCE NOTES BUTTON ON THE STANDARD TOOLBAR.

OR...
- RIGHT-CLICK THE RESOURCE AND SELECT RESOURCE NOTES.

Project's Scheduling Formula
Duration x Units = Work

Figure 3-7. The scheduling formula is the basis for Project's scheduling calculations.

Before diving into how to assign resources to tasks, it's important to understand the scheduling relationship between tasks and resources. Project schedules its tasks with *effort-driven scheduling*, which means that it tries to calculate the amount of effort, or work, required to complete a task. Project uses the scheduling formula, as shown in Figure 3-7, to do this.

 You can turn off effort-driven scheduling for every new task that you create. Select Tools → Options *from the menu, click the* Schedule *tab, and uncheck the* New tasks are effort driven *checkbox.*

Let's talk about how this formula is applied using an example. A task is scheduled to last 5 days, or 40 hours. When a resource is assigned to apply 100% of its working time on the task, the scheduling formula looks like this:

40 hours task duration × 100% resource units = 40 hours of work

Now Project knows that the task requires 40 hours of work to be completed.

Changing one of the variables in the formula affects another part of the formula. For example, what if you assigned another resource to work full-time on the task? The duration of the task would change:

20 hours task duration × 200% resource units = 40 hours of work

Thus, once assignments are created between tasks and resources, you as the project manager must understand how changing the variables of the scheduling formula affect other parts of the project.

Assigning Resources to Tasks

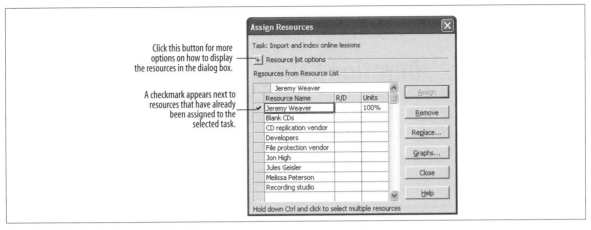

Click this button for more options on how to display the resources in the dialog box.

A checkmark appears next to resources that have already been assigned to the selected task.

Figure 3-8. The Assign Resources dialog box.

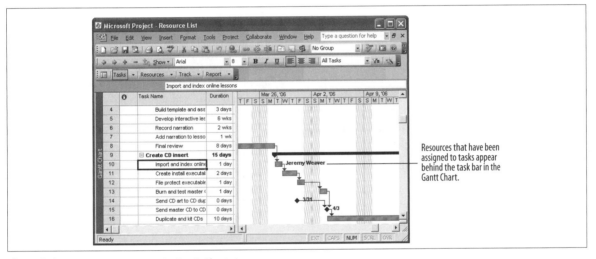

Resources that have been assigned to tasks appear behind the task bar in the Gantt Chart.

Figure 3-9. Resource assignments in Gantt Chart view.

Matching up tasks and resources to do work is called an assignment. Assignments enable your project to move forward and make progress. Technically, you could complete a project without any resources, but resource assignments help you find out valuable information:

- Know who is working on tasks and their availability to work on the task.

- Know if there are enough resources to do the work required in order to finish the project on time.

- Know if certain resources are asked to do too much work on the project; these are called *overallocated resources*.

This lesson will show you how to assign work resources to tasks.

If you choose not to add resources into the resource sheet before you assign them to tasks, select Tools → Options *from the menu and click the* General *tab. Check the* Automatically add new resources *option, and* Project *will add resources into the resource sheet as they are assigned to tasks.*

1 Select View → Gantt Chart from the menu.

This is a good view in which to assign resources to tasks.

Let's assign a resource to the "Import and index online lessons" task.

2 Select the Import and index online lessons task. Click the Assign Resources button on the Standard toolbar.

The Assign Resources dialog box appears. All you have to do is select the resource you want to use for the task.

Assign Jeremy Weaver to this task.

> **TIP**
> *Did you know you can replace one resource with another? Just select the task whose resource you want to replace and press the* Assign Resources button. *Then, in the* Assign Resources dialog box, select the assigned resource, click the Replace button, select a new resource(s), and click OK.*

3 Select the Jeremy Weaver resource from the Resource List in the dialog box. Click the Assign button.

A checkmark appears next to the Jeremy Weaver resource, as shown in Figure 3-8.

Notice that Jeremy is able to devote 100% of his time to the project, as shown under the Units field. This is the information you entered when you created the resource.

4 Click the Close button.

Jeremy has been assigned to the "Import and index online lessons" task. You can view a task's resource in the chart area of the view.

5 Click the Go To Selected Task button on the Standard toolbar.

To view the resource assignment, scroll to the right until you see the end of the task bar for the "Import and index online lessons" task, as shown in

Figure 3-9. The name of the resource assigned to the task is listed at the end of the task bar.

Let's create another resource assignment.

6 Select the Record narration task. Click the Assign Resources button on the Standard toolbar.

The Assign Resources dialog box appears.

7 Select the Jules Geisler resource from the Resource List in the dialog box. Click the Assign button.

A checkmark appears next to the assigned resource. But this time, notice that 50% appears in the Units field. This indicates that Jules is available to work on the project part-time.

8 Click the Close button.

The dialog box closes.

Notice that even though the Jules Geisler resource is only going to be available to work on the project part-time (50%), the duration of the "Record narration" task does not change; it remains at two weeks. That doesn't seem to make sense with effort-driven scheduling: if she's only working part-time on the task, why doesn't the task duration double?

The reason is that the scheduling formula is calculated for the first time when an assignment is created. So right now the scheduling formula for Task 6 looks like this:

80 hours task duration (two weeks) × 50% resource units = 40 hours work

Project has no reason to believe that this is a problem. But you know that there is a problem: the task really takes 80 hours of work. To adjust the scheduling formula and increase the hours of work, change the duration of the task:

80 hours task duration (four weeks) × 50% resource units = 80 hours work

Does this relationship make sense? If not, you'll get another dose of this effort-driven scheduling rigmarole in the next lesson, when you see what happens when you assign additional resources to a project.

QUICK REFERENCE

TO ASSIGN RESOURCES:

1. VIEW THE PROJECT IN GANTT CHART VIEW.

2. SELECT A TASK AND CLICK THE ASSIGN RESOURCES BUTTON ON THE STANDARD TOOLBAR.

3. SELECT THE RESOURCE YOU WANT TO ASSIGN FROM THE RESOURCE LIST IN THE DIALOG BOX.

4. CLICK THE ASSIGN BUTTON.

5. CLICK THE CLOSE BUTTON TO CLOSE THE ASSIGN RESOURCES DIALOG BOX.

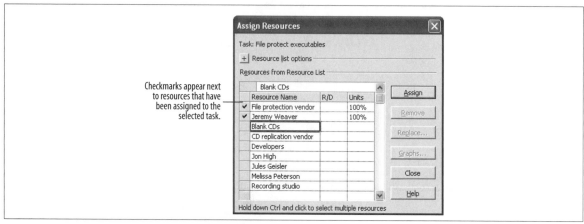

Checkmarks appear next to resources that have been assigned to the selected task.

Figure 3-10. The Assign Resources dialog box.

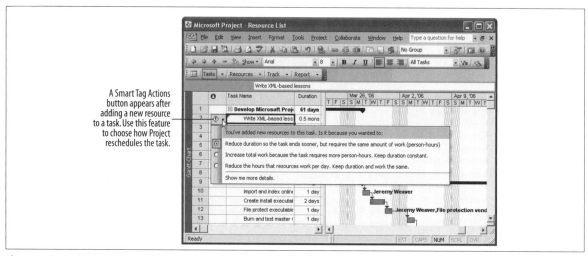

A Smart Tag Actions button appears after adding a new resource to a task. Use this feature to choose how Project reschedules the task.

Figure 3-11. Adding resource assignments in Gantt Chart view.

It is inevitable that you will need to assign multiple resources to a task at some point in your project. But it is very important to understand exactly what you are doing when you assign multiple resources. There are two ways to assign multiple resources to a task:

- **Assign multiple resources when the assignment is created.** This does not affect the task duration: it affects only the scheduled hours of work for the task.

TIP

To assign multiple resources to a task without changing the task's original duration, make sure all the resources are selected when resources are first assigned to the task. Doing so will ensure that the task duration is not affected.

- **Assign additional resources after the assignment is created.** This affects task duration: with more resource units available to do the scheduled hours of work, the task duration decreases.

This lesson will show you what happens to scheduling in your project when you assign multiple resources in each of these ways.

1 Select the File protect executables task.

Notice that the task is scheduled to last one day.

You want two resources to work together to complete this task: Jeremy Weaver and the File protection vendor.

2 Click the Assign Resources button on the Standard toolbar.

Since you know which resources must work on this task, select and assign them to the task at the same time.

3 Select the Jeremy Weaver resource from the Resource List in the dialog box. Press and hold the Ctrl key and select the File protection vendor resource.

Both resources are selected, as shown in Figure 3-10, so you can create the assignment.

4 Click the Assign button. Click the Close button.

Two resources appear after the task, and the task duration remains at one day.

Right now, the scheduling formula for the task looks like this:

$$8 \text{ hours task duration (1 day)} \times 200\% \text{ assignment units} = 16 \text{ hours work}$$

Remember that the 200% assignment units come from two resources at 100%.

The results are very different when you assign additional resources to a task. Let's try it.

5 Click the Write XML-based lessons task.

First, let's create a resource assignment for the task.

6 Click the Assign Resources button on the Standard toolbar.

The Assign Resources dialog box appears.

7 Select the Jon High resource from the Resource List in the dialog box. Click the Assign button and click Close.

An assignment has been created for the task. Here's what the scheduling formula looks like:

$$160 \text{ hours task duration (1 month)} \times 100\% \text{ assignment units} = 160 \text{ hours work}$$

What happens if you increase the assignment units working on the task by assigning another resource to the task?

8 Click the Assign Resources button on the standard toolbar.

The Assign Resources dialog box appears.

9 Select the Melissa Peterson resource from the Resource List in the dialog box. Click the Assign button and click Close.

Notice that the duration of the task is cut in half: from 1 month to 0.5 months, or 2 weeks.

The schedule formula changed. Now that there are more resources available to do the work, the duration of the task decreased.

$$80 \text{ hours task duration (0.5 month)} \times 200\% \text{ assignment units} = 160 \text{ hours work}$$

Notice the Smart Tag Actions button that appears next to the task, as shown in Figure 3-11. This button allows you to specify how Project reschedules the task. For example, you could keep the duration the same but increase work hours, or reduce the number of hours the resources work on the task each day.

Hopefully, you now have a better understanding of how assignments affect the way the project is scheduled. As long as you understand the schedule formula, you shouldn't have any problems creating and managing assignments in your project.

QUICK REFERENCE

TO ASSIGN MULTIPLE RESOURCES:

1. SELECT THE TASK AND CLICK THE ASSIGN RESOURCES BUTTON ON THE STANDARD TOOLBAR.

2. SELECT THE RESOURCES YOU WANT TO ASSIGN FROM THE RESOURCE LIST IN THE DIALOG BOX.

3. CLICK THE ASSIGN BUTTON.

4. CLICK THE CLOSE BUTTON TO CLOSE THE ASSIGN RESOURCES DIALOG BOX.

TO ASSIGN ADDITIONAL RESOURCES:

1. SELECT THE TASK TO WHICH YOU WANT TO ADD A RESOURCE, AND CLICK THE ASSIGN RESOURCES BUTTON ON THE STANDARD TOOLBAR.

2. IN THE DIALOG BOX, SELECT THE RESOURCE YOU WANT TO ADD TO THE ASSIGNMENT.

3. CLICK THE ASSIGN BUTTON AND CLICK THE CLOSE BUTTON.

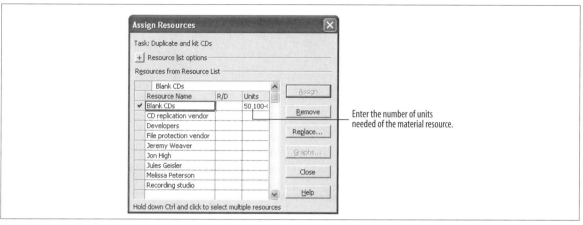

Figure 3-12. The Assign Resources dialog box with material resource assignments.

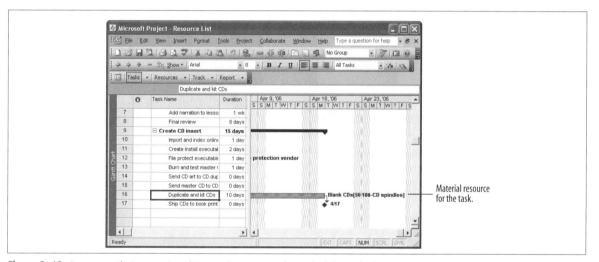

Figure 3-13. Resources that are assigned to a task appear at the end of the task's bar.

It's good to assign material resources to tasks so you can see how much material you are using and at what cost. Assigning a material resource to a task isn't very different from assigning a work resource. The main difference is that you have to enter the amount of the resource that will be used, rather than the resource availability.

1 Select the Duplicate and kit CDs task and click the Assign Resources button.

The Assign Resources dialog box appears.

2 Select the Blank CDs resource from the Resource List in the dialog box, as shown in Figure 3-12.

Notice that the material label you entered when you created the resource (100-CD spindles) is used to indicate the number of units scheduled to be consumed.

3 Click the Assign button.

You have assigned the "Blank CDs" resource to the task, but you must also enter the number of resource units needed. Enter that number in the Units field.

4 Click the Units field, type 50 and press Enter.

Right now, you are planning on duplicating 5,000 CDs when working on the "Duplicate and kit CDs" task.

5 Click the Close button.

The material resource is assigned to the task, as shown in Figure 3-13.

QUICK REFERENCE

TO ASSIGN A MATERIAL RESOURCE:

1. SELECT A TASK. CLICK THE ASSIGN RESOURCES BUTTON.

2. SELECT THE MATERIAL RESOURCE(S) FOR THE TASK.

3. ENTER HOW MANY UNITS OF EACH RESOURCE YOU NEED.

4. CLICK THE ASSIGN BUTTON AND CLICK CLOSE.

Chapter Three Review

Lesson Summary

Entering People Resources

To Open Resource Sheet View: Select View → Resource Sheet from the menu.

To Enter a People Resource: Click in the Resource Name field and enter a name for the resource. Click in the Max. Units field and enter the resource's availability to the project, and then click in the Std. Rate field and enter the pay rate for the resource.

Entering Equipment Resources

To Enter an Equipment Resource: Click in the Resource Name field and enter a name for the resource. Click in the Max. Units field and enter the resource's availability to the project, and then click in the Std. Rate field and enter the cost of the resource.

Entering Material Resources

To Enter a Material Resource: Click in the Resource Name field and enter a name for the resource. Click the Type field list arrow and select Material from the list. Click in the Material Label field and enter the material resource's unit of measurement, and then click in the Std. Rate field and enter the rate for the resource.

Adjusting Individual Resource Working Schedules

To Adjust an Individual Resource Working Schedule: Select the resource and select Project → Resource Information from the menu, or click the Resource Information button on the Standard toolbar, or press Shift + F2. Edit the working time for the resource in the dialog box.

Using Resource Notes

To Enter a Resource Note: Click the Resource Notes button on the Standard toolbar, or right-click the resource and select Resource Notes.

Understanding Effort-Driven Project Scheduling

Be able to understand the scheduling relationship between tasks and resources in a project.

Assigning Resources to Tasks

To Assign Resources: Make sure you are in Gantt Chart view, and then select a task and click the Assign Resources button on the Standard toolbar. Select the resource you want to assign from the Resource List in the dialog box and click the Assign button. Click the Close button to close the dialog box.

Assigning Additional Resources to Tasks

To Assign Multiple Resources: Select the task and click the Assign Resources button on the Standard toolbar. Select the resources you want to assign from the Resource List in the dialog box and click the Assign button. Click the Close button to close the dialog box.

To Assign Additional Resources: Select the task to which you want to add a resource, and click the Assign Resources button on the Standard toolbar. Select the resource you want to add to the assignment, click the Assign button, and click the Close button when you're finished.

Assigning Material Resources to Tasks

To Assign a Material Resource: Select a task and click the Assign Resources button. Select the material resource(s) for the task and enter how many units of each resource you need. Click the Assign button and click Close.

Quiz

1. What are the two types of resources?

   A. Work and Cost.

   B. Work and Written.

   C. Work and Material.

   D. Oil and Coal.

2. You can't change the working calendar for just one single resource. (True or False?)

3. You should track equipment that (select all that apply):

   A. accumulates cost.

   B. was donated to you by an external resource.

   C. is shared.

   D. is worth more than $10,000.

4. Material resources are:

   A. resources that are made of fabric.

   B. selfish resources.

   C. expensive resources.

   D. the goods needed by work resources in order to complete tasks.

5. Which of the following formulas is Project's Scheduling Formula?

   A. Units × Work = Duration

   B. Duration × Units = Work

   C. Work × Duration = Units

   D. Duration × Work = Units

6. You can't assign more than one resource to a task. (True or False?)

Homework

1. Start Microsoft Project 2003.

2. Navigate to your practice files and open the Homework 3 project.

3. Switch to Resource Sheet view, and add a work resource named "Mom" who works for $0.50 an hour.

4. Select resource #1, select Project → Resource Information from the menu, click the Working Time tab, and change the resource's working schedule so that

Snoogie is only working from 8:00a.m. to 12:00p.m. on January 31, 2003.

5. Give resource #8, "pitcher," a Std. rate of $0.75/hr.

6. Switch back to Gantt Chart view. Select task #20 and assign the work resource "Bill Gates" to it.

7. Select task #13 and assign the material resources "Grade A Sunkist Lemons (10 lbs.)" and "Crystal Refined Sugar (2.5 5-lb. bags)" to the task.

8. Close Homework 3 without saving your changes.

Quiz Answers

1. C. The two types of resources are work and material.

2. False. You can change a single resource's working calendar.

3. A and C. You don't have to track every piece of equipment that is used in a project, but you should keep track of equipment that accumulates cost or is shared.

4. D. Material resources are the goods needed by work resources to complete tasks.

5. B. The correct formula is Duration × Units = Work.

6. False. You *can* assign more than one resource to a task.

CHAPTER 4
VIEWING THE PROJECT

CHAPTER OBJECTIVES:

Use split views, Lesson 4.1

View sorted and grouped information, Lessons 4.2 and 4.3

Use filters and AutoFilters, Lessons 4.4 and 4.5

View task or resource details, Lesson 4.6

Use the Zoom feature, Lesson 4.7

Prerequisites

• **Have a project with tasks, resources, and costs.**

• **Understand project management.**

One of Project's best attributes is that it lets you view project information from dozens of different angles. This chapter is pretty cut-and-dry; it shows you some common ways to view various aspects of the project's information, such as resource overallocation, the critical path, and task or resource details. This chapter also shows you different ways to organize information with filters, groups, and fields.

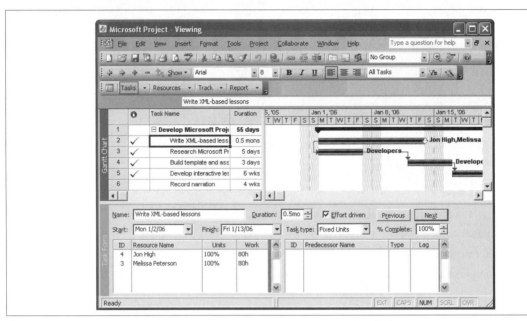

Figure 4-1. A split view with Gantt Chart view on top and the Task Form view on the bottom.

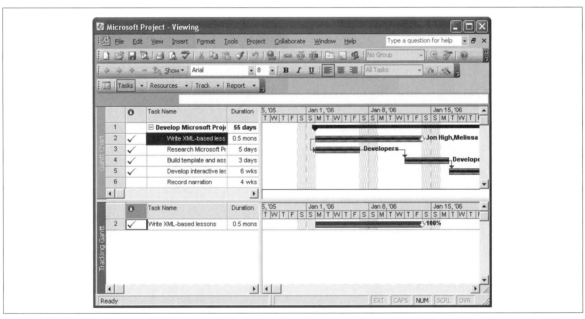

Figure 4-2. A split view with Gantt Chart view on top and Tracking Gantt view on the bottom.

You may find that a single view does not display all the information you want to see. In these instances, a *split view* might be the solution to your problem. A split view displays two views of the project in the same window. For example, you could display Gantt Chart view in the top half of the window and Task Form view in the bottom, to view detailed information about a selected task.

This lesson will show you how to use a split view.

1 Navigate to your Practice folder and open Lesson 4. Save the file as Viewing.

Some views are created to be split, such as Resource Allocation view.

2 Select the Write XML-based lessons task and select Window → Split from the menu.

The window splits in two, and more information about the selected task is shown in the bottom half of the window, as shown in Figure 4-1.

Notice that the bottom view isn't a view you've seen before. This is Task Form view, which is the default view when a window is split. It displays more information on the task or resource that is selected in the top view. Right-click the Task Form view to see different information about the selected resource or task.

3 Click in the bottom pane of the window.

To display a different view in the pane, you must first select it.

4 Select View → Tracking Gantt from the menu.

The Tracking Gantt view is displayed in the bottom pane, as shown in Figure 4-2.

The Tracking Gantt view in the bottom pane displays the task and the amount of work performed on the task.

As you begin tracking and making changes to your project, you will find splitting views to be more useful.

5 Select Window → Remove Split from the menu.

QUICK REFERENCE

TO SPLIT A VIEW

1. SELECT WINDOW → SPLIT FROM THE MENU.

2. CLICK IN THE BOTTOM PANE AND SELECT THE VIEW YOU WANT TO DISPLAY.

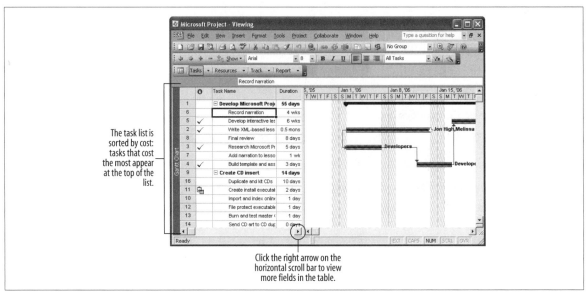

The task list is sorted by cost: tasks that cost the most appear at the top of the list.

Click the right arrow on the horizontal scroll bar to view more fields in the table.

Figure 4-3. The sorted project.

Tasks and resources appear in ID-number order in Project by default. However, you can change this by sorting them; sorting lets you rearrange the order in which tasks and resources appear.

1 Select Project → Sort → by Cost from the menu.

The project tasks that cost the most appear at the top of the list, as shown in Figure 4-3.

⟩ NOTE ⟨   *If you want to see the Cost field for the tasks, use the Task Entry table's horizontal scroll bar to scroll through the available fields.*

Now let's return to the default sort type: by ID.

2 Select Project → Sort → by ID from the menu.

The project is displayed so that the task IDs are in descending order.

Sorting resources isn't much different from sorting tasks. The only difference is that you can use different sorting types.

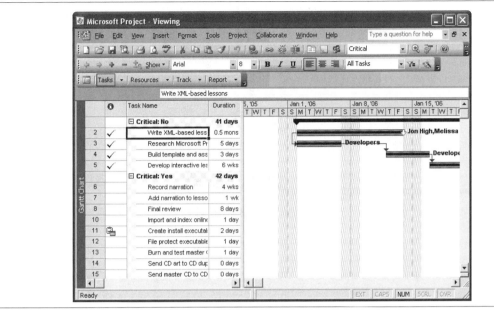

Figure 4-4. Results of a critical task grouping.

We touched on sorting tasks and resources in the previous lesson, but this lesson will concentrate solely on grouping. Grouping is a handy organizational tool, allowing you to focus on a variety of project angles. This lesson focuses on grouping tasks, but you can group resources the same way.

1 Select Project → Group by: → Critical from the menu.

The tasks on the Gantt Chart are now grouped by tasks that are critical and tasks that are not critical, as shown in Figure 4-4. The group headings are highlighted in yellow.

2 Click the ⊟ collapse button in the yellow Critical: No heading.

The tasks that are not critical are collapsed, so that the critical tasks are easier to see.

Now go back to the default Gantt Chart task order.

3 Select Project → Group by: → No Group from the menu.

You are now back to your default view.

Who knew there were so many ways to group the project's tasks? Grouping resources is done the same way, but in a resource view instead of a task view.

QUICK REFERENCE

TO VIEW GROUPED INFORMATION:

1. SELECT PROJECT → GROUP BY: FROM THE MENU.

2. CHOOSE A GROUPING OPTION FROM THE MENU.

TO RETURN TO THE DEFAULT VIEW:

• SELECT PROJECT → GROUP BY: → NO GROUP FROM THE MENU.

Filtering Information

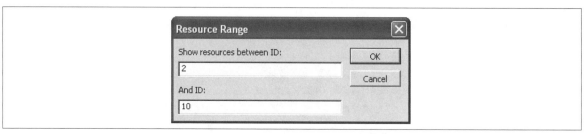

Figure 4-5. The Resource Range dialog box.

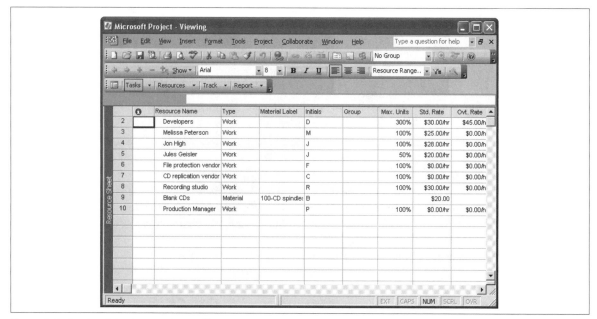

Figure 4-6. Results of the Resource Range filter.

By *filtering* a list, you display only the records that meet your criteria, and hide the records that do not. There are several ways to filter your lists. This lesson focuses on how to filter resources, but you can filter tasks the same way.

1 **Select** View → Resource Sheet **from the menu.**

The project displays all the resources involved in the project.

2 **Select** Project → Filtered for: **from the menu.**

A list of all the different types of filters you can choose from appears.

Most filters are already created; all you have to do is select the filter to view the criteria it is supposed to find. For example, to view all the milestones in the project, select the Milestones task filter.

Let's use an interactive filter in this lesson.

3 Select Resource Range from the Filter menu.

The Resource Range dialog box appears. Specify the range you want to view in the dialog box.

4 Type 2 in the first text box, press Tab, and type 10 in the second text box.

Compare your dialog box to Figure 4-5.

5 Click OK.

The filtered resources appear, as shown in Figure 4-6.

Now, turn the filter off by applying a highlighting filter.

6 Select Project → Filtered for: → All Resources from the menu.

You are back to the default view with no filters.

QUICK REFERENCE

TO VIEW FILTERED INFORMATION:

- SELECT PROJECT → FILTERED FOR: FROM THE MENU, AND THEN CHOOSE THE FILTER TYPE YOU WANT TO USE.

TO TURN A FILTER OFF:

- SELECT PROJECT → FILTERED FOR: → ALL TASKS OR ALL RESOURCES FROM THE MENU.

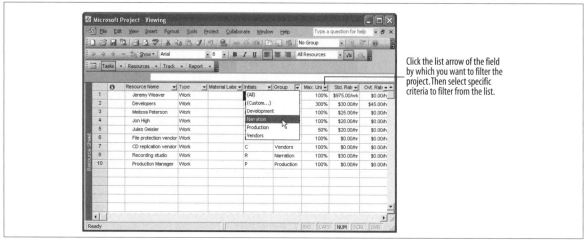

Figure 4-7. Click the column heading list arrow and select the criteria you want to use for the filter.

Click the list arrow of the field by which you want to filter the project. Then select specific criteria to filter from the list.

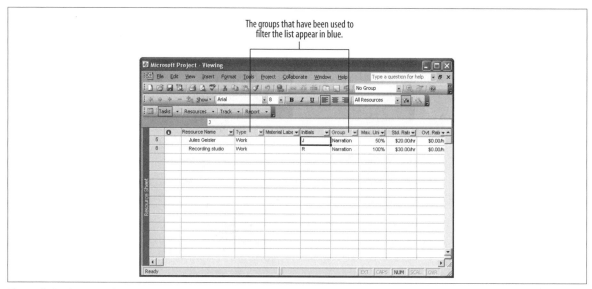

The groups that have been used to filter the list appear in blue.

Figure 4-8. The AutoFilter using Type and Group criteria.

AutoFilters are a more advanced type of filter that use features from both interactive and highlighting filter types. With AutoFilters, you can filter information by each field in a view.

1 **Make sure the project is in** Resource Sheet **view.**

You can use AutoFilter with tasks or resources, but we'll use resources for this lesson.

2 **Select** Project → **Filtered for:** → **AutoFilter from the menu.**

All of the resources remain on the screen, but look at the top row that contains all the field headings: list arrows appear on the right side of the headings. These lists include each entry in the field.

3 Click the Resource Name list arrow.

A list of all the resource names drops down. Other columns don't have as many entries.

4 Click outside the Resource Name list to close it.

Try another field.

5 Click the Type list arrow.

Only four entries appear: Work, Material, All, and Custom.

6 Select Work from the list.

Only the work resources appear in the project window. Notice that the Type heading appears in blue, indicating that is has been used as filter criteria.

AutoFilters are useful because they are easy to use, especially if you are searching for specific information. For example, you can filter the material list you just created so it is even more specific.

7 Click the Group list arrow. Select Narration from the list, as shown in Figure 4-7.

Now the project is filtered so that the only resources shown are work resources used for narration, as shown in Figure 4-8.

When you're done, don't forget to turn off the AutoFilter…

8 Select Project → Filtered for: → AutoFilter from the menu.

The filters you specified are turned off, and all the resources are shown once again.

QUICK REFERENCE

TO USE THE AUTOFILTER:

1. SELECT PROJECT → FILTERED FOR: → AUTOFILTER FROM THE MENU.

2. CLICK THE LIST ARROW OF THE FIELD BY WHICH YOU WANT TO FILTER THE PROJECT.

3. FROM THE LIST, SELECT THE CRITERIA BY WHICH YOU WANT TO FILTER THE PROJECT.

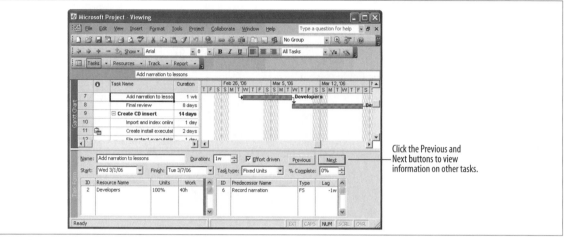

Click the Previous and
Next buttons to view
information on other tasks.

Figure 4-9. The Project screen split between Gantt Chart view and Task Entry view.

Because Project is so powerful, it's easy to lose track of who is assigned to what task and the amount of time the task will take. It can sometimes be hard to quickly find information for a task and its resources. This lesson will show you a way to make this information more readily available.

1 Select View → Gantt Chart **from the menu.**

Let's select a task and view its details.

2 Select the Add narration to lessons **task.**

Now let's view the details for this task.

3 Select View → More Views **from the menu.**

The More Views dialog box appears.

4 Select Task Entry **and click** Apply.

The Task Form appears in the lower half of the Project window, as shown in Figure 4-9. In this lower window, notice that you can see task details such as assigned resources, start and finish dates, and predecessors.

5 Select Window → Remove Split **from the menu.**

The Task Form disappears, and the Gantt Chart appears in the entire window.

QUICK REFERENCE

TO VIEW DETAILS FOR A TASK OR RESOURCE:

1. SELECT THE TASK OR RESOURCE.
2. SELECT VIEW → MORE VIEWS FROM THE MENU.
3. SELECT TASK ENTRY OR RESOURCE ENTRY AND CLICK APPLY.

Using Zoom

Figure 4-10. The Zoom dialog box.

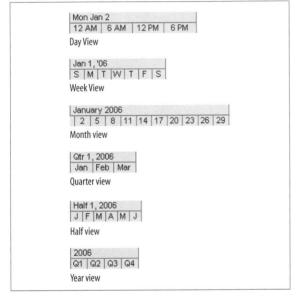

Figure 4-11. Various Zoom options as they appear on the timescale.

When you are viewing and working with a project, you may want to look at things from a smaller or larger perspective. Project makes it easy for you to do this with its handy Zoom tool. For example, you can zoom in on a

project to view everything by day, or you can zoom out to view everything by month.

1 Select the Write XML-based lessons task and select View → Zoom from the menu.

The Zoom dialog box appears, as shown in Figure 4-10. Let's zoom in on this task.

2 Select the Selected task option and click OK.

The selected task appears in the chart. Notice the timescale located directly above the bar chart. It has adjusted itself so that you can see the entire duration of the task on the screen. See how the timescale adjusts itself for the various views in Figure 4-11.

Let's switch back to the previous view.

3 Select View → Zoom from the menu and select the Custom option. Type 23 in the first box, and then click inside the second box and select Day(s) from the list.

You now return to Week view. You can also zoom in or out of a project by using the Zoom buttons on the Standard toolbar.

4 Click the 🔍 Zoom Out button on the Standard toolbar.

Your project switches to Month view. Let's return to the previous view.

⋛ NOTE ⋛   Click the ⏷ Toolbar Options button and select the Zoom Out button from the menu if you don't see the Zoom Out button on the Standard toolbar.

5 Click the 🔍 Zoom In button on the Standard toolbar.

Zooming in or out of a project is all about personal preference. Experiment with the different views until you find one that works best for you *and* your project.

QUICK REFERENCE

TO ZOOM INTO A PROJECT:

- CLICK THE ZOOM IN BUTTON ON THE STANDARD TOOLBAR.

TO ZOOM OUT OF A PROJECT:

- CLICK THE ZOOM OUT BUTTON ON THE STANDARD TOOLBAR.

TO DISPLAY THE ZOOM DIALOG BOX:

- SELECT VIEW → ZOOM FROM THE MENU.

Chapter Four Review

Lesson Summary

Using Split Views

To Split a View: Select Window → Split from the menu. Click in the bottom pane and select the view you want to display.

Sorting Information

To View Sorted Information: Select Project → Sort, and then choose a sorting option.

To Cancel a Sort: Select Project → Sort → by ID to return to the default sort.

Grouping Information

To View Grouped Information: Select Project → Group by: from the menu and choose a grouping option from the menu.

To Return to the Default View: Select Project → Group by: → No Group from the menu.

Filtering Information

To View Filtered Information: Select Project → Filtered for: from the menu and then choose the filter type you want to use.

To Turn a Filter Off: Select Project → Filtered for: → All Tasks or All Resources from the menu.

Using AutoFilters

To Use the AutoFilter: Select Project → Filtered For: → AutoFilter from the menu. Click the list arrow of the field by which you want to filter the project and then, from that list, select the criteria by which you want to filter the project.

Viewing Details

To View Details for a Task or Resource: Select the task or resource and select View → More Views from the menu. Select Task Entry or Resource Entry and click Apply. The Task Form will appear below the Gantt Chart, with details about the task or resource.

Using Zoom

To Zoom In or Out of a Project: Click the Zoom In button on the Standard toolbar to zoom in. Click the Zoom Out button on the Standard toolbar to zoom out.

To Display the Zoom Dialog Box: Select View → Zoom from the menu.

Quiz

1. You can't display more than one view at a time. (True or False?)

2. Tasks and resources appear in a specific order that cannot be changed. (True or False?)

3. To view grouped information:
   A. Click the View Grouped Information button on the Standard toolbar.
   B. Select View → Project → Groups from the menu.
   C. Select Project → Group by: from the menu and choose a grouping option.
   D. Select Project → Grouping from the menu and choose a grouping option.

4. Which of these is NOT a way in which to view information?
   A. Filtering
   B. Sifting
   C. Grouping
   D. Sorting

5. To find information quickly about a task or resource:
   A. Click the task or resource as fast as you can.
   B. Triple-click the task or resource.
   C. Filter the project by the task or resource you want to find information on.
   D. View the task or resource's details.

Homework

1. Start Microsoft Project 2003.

2. Navigate to your practice files and open the Homework 4 project.

3. Split the project window so that the Gantt Chart is in the upper half of the window and the Task Form is in the bottom half of the window.

4. Sort the Gantt Chart by finish date.

5. Filter the Gantt Chart for summary tasks.

6. Zoom out to view your project by Quarter.

7. Close Homework 4 without saving any changes.

Quiz Answers

1. False. You can display two views at the same time using the split view feature.

2. False. Tasks and resources appear in ID number order by default, but you can change this by sorting.

3. C. To view grouped information, select Project → Group by: from the menu and choose a grouping option.

4. B. There is no such thing as sifting information in Project.

5. D. To find information quickly regarding a task or resource, view the task or resource's details.

CHAPTER 5

WORKING WITH TASKS

CHAPTER OBJECTIVES:

Overlap tasks, Lesson 5.1

Delay tasks, Lesson 5.2

Set task deadlines, Lesson 5.3

Set task constraints, Lesson 5.4

Split tasks, Lesson 5.5

Understand task type, Lesson 5.6

Assign a new calendar to a task, Lesson 5.7

Understand task indicators, Lesson 5.8

Prerequisites

- **Have a project in which you have already entered tasks.**
- **Understand project management.**

Most of your time working with tasks will be spent creating a task list, linking tasks, and assigning resources to tasks. You could successfully manage a project using only these task properties, but there are many other useful ways to work with tasks.

This chapter will show you some advanced task properties you can work with to further refine the scheduling of your project. For example, you can change the start dates of dependent tasks by overlapping and delaying task relationships, and take scheduling matters into your own hands by defining the start or end dates of a task using constraints. Project still does all the calculating for you, but now you'll learn how to control how much of that calculating takes place.

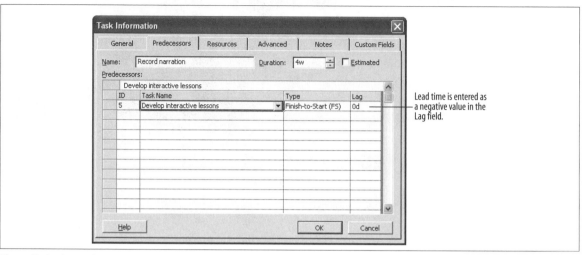

Figure 5-1. The Predecessors tab in the Task Information dialog box.

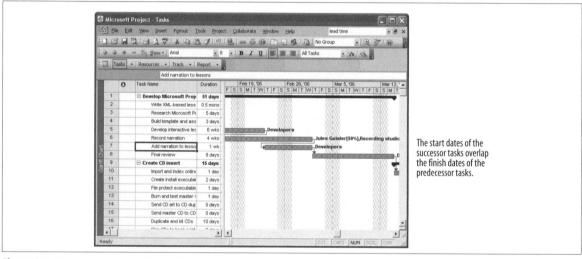

Figure 5-2. Overlapped tasks with lead time.

Overlapping linked tasks means that you want the successor task to begin before the predecessor task ends. Therefore, you give the successor task *lead time*. Lead time can be entered as a duration or as a task completion percentage.

1 Navigate to your Practice folder and open Lesson 5. Save the file as Tasks.

Right now, the "Record narration" task is scheduled to start when the "Develop interactive lessons" task is

finished. But really, the narrator can begin to record narration when about half of the lessons are done.

2 Select the Record narration task. Click the Task Information button on the Standard toolbar.

The Task Information dialog box appears, as shown in Figure 5-1.

3 Click the Predecessors tab.

The predecessor task appears in the Predecessors list.

4 Click the Lag field and type -50%.

When you are entering lead time for a task, make sure it is a negative (-) value. Otherwise, Project 2003 will think you are entering lag time.

This means the "Record narration" task will start when the "Develop interactive lessons" task is 50% complete.

⁝ NOTE ⁝ *Lead time works differently with different types of links. For example, in a Start-to-Start relationship with three days lead time, the successor task would start three days before the predecessor.*

5 Click OK.

The start date of the "Record narration" task is rescheduled.

The "Add narration to lessons" task is scheduled to begin when the "Record narration" task is finished, but the developers can add narration to lessons that have already been recorded. Let's try another way to add lead time to a task relationship.

6 Double-click the link line connecting the "Record narration" and "Add narration to lessons" tasks.

The Task Dependency dialog box appears.

7 Click the Lag field and type -1 week.

This means the "Add narration to lessons" task will start one week before the "Record narration" task is complete.

8 Click OK.

Project reschedules the start dates of the tasks, as shown in Figure 5-2.

QUICK REFERENCE

TO OVERLAP TASKS:

1. SELECT THE SUCCESSOR TASK YOU WANT TO OVERLAP.

2. CLICK THE TASK INFORMATION BUTTON ON THE STANDARD TOOLBAR.

3. CLICK THE PREDECESSORS TAB.

4. CLICK IN THE LAG FIELD AND ENTER THE LEAD TIME AS A NEGATIVE (-) VALUE.

OR...

1. DOUBLE-CLICK THE LINK LINE CONNECTING THE TASKS.

2. CLICK IN THE LAG FIELD AND ENTER THE LEAD TIME AS A NEGATIVE (-) VALUE.

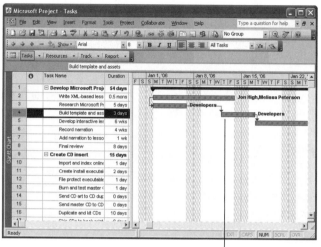

The start date of the task is delayed by the amount of lag time entered for the task.

Figure 5-3. Delayed tasks with lag time.

Delaying a task means that there will be some time between the end of a predecessor task and the beginning of a successor task. Therefore, you give the predecessor task *lag time*. Working with lag time is like working with lead time, except that lag time is a positive value. It can be entered as a duration or as a task completion percentage.

Let's delay the start of the "Build template and assets" task by a few days.

1 Select the Build template and assets **task. Click the** Task Information button **on the Standard toolbar.**

The Task Information dialog box appears.

2 Click the Predecessors **tab.**

The predecessor task appears in the Predecessors list.

3 Click the Lag **field and type** 3 days.

This means the "Build template and assets" task will start three days after the "Research Microsoft Project 2003" task is finished.

4 Click OK.

The start date of the "Build template and assets" task is rescheduled, as shown in Figure 5-3.

Setting Task Deadlines

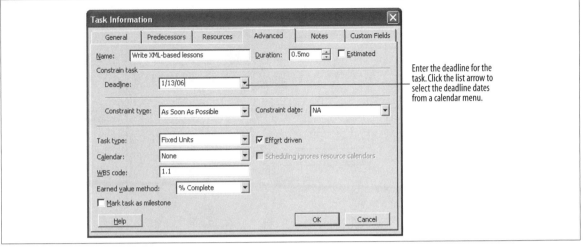

Enter the deadline for the task. Click the list arrow to select the deadline dates from a calendar menu.

Figure 5-4. The Advanced tab of the Task Information dialog box.

Deadlines are very helpful in project management, because they help Project indicate whether a task has been completed on schedule. It's important to understand that setting a deadline doesn't affect how tasks are scheduled; instead, the deadline is more like an indicator of the scheduling status of the project.

1 Select the Write XML-based lessons task.

Adding a deadline is a good way to keep track of how the task is going.

2 Click the Task Information button on the Standard toolbar.

The task is scheduled to finish on 1/13/06. Let's add a deadline to make sure that's when the task ends.

3 Click the Advanced tab.

This tab is where you can define advanced task properties, such as deadlines.

4 Click the Deadline box and type 1/13/06.

Compare your dialog box to Figure 5-4.

5 Click OK.

A small green deadline arrow appears on the task's bar.

So what happens once the deadline for a task is set? Project continues to update the task as work progresses.

If the task is finished by the deadline date, nothing happens and the project continues as scheduled.

If the task finishes *after* the deadline date, an ◆ indicator appears next to the task, notifying you that the task is scheduled to finish after its deadline. When this happens, you can choose to work with the task to make it finish on time, or simply allow the project to continue as scheduled and ignore the indicator.

QUICK REFERENCE

TO ENTER A DEADLINE:

1. SELECT THE TASK.
2. CLICK THE TASK INFORMATION BUTTON ON THE STANDARD TOOLBAR.
3. CLICK THE ADVANCED TAB.
4. ENTER THE DEADLINE DATE IN THE DEADLINE BOX.
5. CLICK OK.

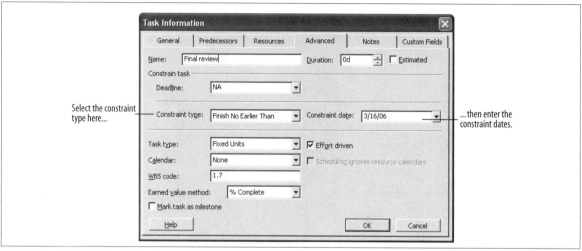

Select the constraint type here...

...then enter the constraint dates.

Figure 5-5. The Advanced tab of the Task Information dialog box.

Task constraints are a way to control and define task schedules, overwriting Project's effort-driven scheduling plans if necessary. Each type of constraint is used differently, but all of them should be used wisely. Constraints have a definite effect on the scheduling of the project.

≂ NOTE ≂ *Task constraints should be used sparingly: misuse of constraints restricts Project's ability to calculate and schedule tasks efficiently. For example, if you set an inflexible constraint for the start date of a task and its predecessor ends early, Project cannot reschedule the task and take advantage of this extra time.*

1 Select the Final review **task.**

Let's add a constraint so that the "Final review" task does not end before the scheduled finish date: 3/16/06. Doing this means the successor task will definitely start on its scheduled start date.

2 Click the 🖼 Task Information button **on the Standard toolbar. Click the** Advanced **tab.**

The Advanced tab of the Task Information dialog box appears.

3 Click the Constraint type **list arrow and select** Finish No Earlier Than **from the list.**

Finish No Earlier Than is a *moderate* constraint, which means the task cannot be finished before the constraint date.

4 Type 3/16/06 **in the** Constraint date **box.**

Once the constraint information is entered, as shown in Figure 5-5, complete the constraint.

5 Click OK.

The dialog box closes, and the constraint is set. A constraint indicator also appears next to the task.

 A constraint indicator appears next to a task with a constraint. Hold your cursor over it to view more information about the constraint.

There are quite a few different types of constraints you can use in the project. It is important to know that the constraints are made to work with projects that are scheduled from either the Project Finish Date or the Project Start Date. Typically, applying a constraint to a task in the wrong type of project has undesirable results.

And, of course, don't apply a constraint unless it is unavoidable, such as a deadline that cannot be moved. For more information about constraints, refer to Table 5-1.

Table 5-1. Task Constraints

	Constraint	For Projects Scheduled From	Description
Flexible	As Late As Possible	Project Finish Date	Schedules the latest possible start and finish dates for the task. This is the default constraint for new tasks in projects scheduled from the Project Finish Date.
	As Soon As Possible	Project Start Date	Schedules the earliest possible start and finish dates for the task. This is the default constraint for new tasks in projects scheduled from the Project Start Date.
Moderate	Finish No Earlier Than	Project Start Date	Indicates the earliest possible date that this task can be completed, and the task cannot finish any time before the specified date.
	Finish No Later Than	Project Finish Date	Indicates the latest possible date that this task can be completed, and the task can be finished on or before the specified date.
	Start No Earlier Than	Project Start Date	Indicates the earliest possible date that this task can begin. It cannot start any time before the specified date.
	Start No Later Than	Project Finish Date	Indicates the latest possible date this task can begin. It can start on or before the specified date.
Inflexible	Must Finish On	Inflexible	Indicates the exact date on which a task must finish. Other scheduling parameters—such as task dependencies, lead or lag time, and resource leveling—become secondary to this requirement.
	Must Start On	Inflexible	Indicates the exact date on which a task must begin. Other scheduling parameters—such as task dependencies, lead or lag time, and resource leveling—become secondary to this requirement.

QUICK REFERENCE

TO ENTER A TASK CONSTRAINT:

1. SELECT THE TASK TO WHICH YOU WANT TO ADD A CONSTRAINT.

2. CLICK THE TASK INFORMATION BUTTON ON THE STANDARD TOOLBAR.

3. CLICK THE ADVANCED TAB.

4. CLICK THE CONSTRAINT TYPE LIST ARROW AND SELECT THE CONSTRAINT YOU WANT TO USE.

5. ENTER THE DEADLINE DATE IN THE CONSTRAINT DATE BOX.

6. CLICK OK.

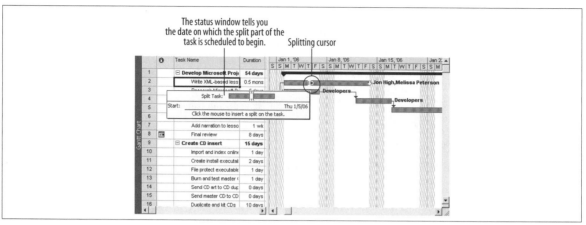

Figure 5-6. Splitting a task.

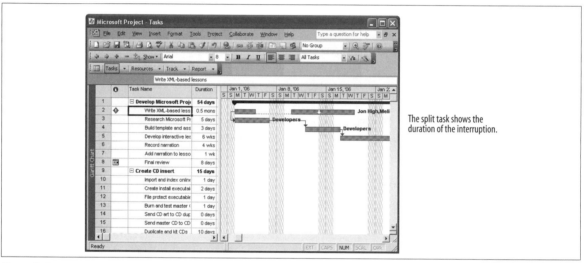

Figure 5-7. The split task.

If work on a task is interrupted, you can split the task to stop work and begin it again at a later date. A task can be split multiple times if necessary.

1 Select the Write XML-based lessons task.

Uh-oh. The resources for this task will have to stop working on this project for a few days to work on another project. We'll have to split the task to account for the time.

2 Click the ⊞ Split Task button on the Standard toolbar.

A status window pops up and the cursor turns into a dividing tool, as shown in Figure 5-6.

3 Place the ‖▸ splitting cursor at 1/05/06.

The instruction window shows the date that the interruption will begin.

4 Click the task bar and drag it to the right until the instruction window says the task will start again on 1/10/06.

A dotted line separates the two parts of the task, as shown in Figure 5-7. The first part of the task ends at 1/05/06, where you began the interruption, and the second part of the task begins at 1/10/06, where you ended the interruption.

Notice that the duration of the task has not changed: it is still 0.5 months. Also notice that a Task Deadline indicator appears next to the task. Since you moved back the finish date of the task, the deadline will not be met.

It is also easy to adjust the length of a split, or to remove the split altogether.

 You can remove a split by dragging one part of the split bar so that it touches another part of the split bar. The task bars will just bond together.

5 Click the second half of the task bar and drag it to the left until the instruction window says the task will start on 1/05/06.

The split is removed, and the task is scheduled to meet its deadline once again.

Notice that the duration of the task never changed; it is still 0.5 (half of a month). Instead, the scheduling of work on the task has changed, moving back the finish date of the task.

QUICK REFERENCE

TO SPLIT A TASK:

1. SELECT THE TASK.
2. CLICK THE SPLIT TASK BUTTON ON THE STANDARD TOOLBAR.
3. PLACE THE SPLITTING CURSOR (⁞↦) ON THE DATE YOU WANT THE INTERRUPTION TO BEGIN.
4. CLICK AND DRAG THE TASK BAR TO THE DATE YOU WANT THE INTERRUPTION TO END.

TO REMOVE A SPLIT:

- CLICK AND DRAG THE SPLIT TASK PORTIONS UNTIL THEY TOUCH.

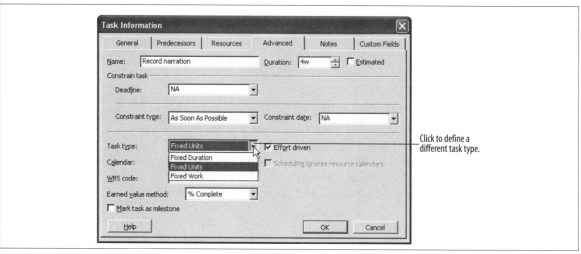

Figure 5-8. The Advanced tab of the Task Information dialog box.

Defining task types changes how tasks are scheduled. For any task, setting the task type determines which part of the scheduling equation Microsoft Project uses to schedule a task. Once a resource assignment is created, tasks are scheduled using this formula:

$$\text{Duration} = \text{Work / Units}$$

The task type changes how this formula is calculated. This lesson will show you more about how task type affects tasks' schedules.

1 Double-click the Record narration task.

The Task Information dialog box appears.

2 Click the Advanced tab in the dialog box.

The Advanced tab appears.

3 Click the Task type list arrow.

A list of the three task type options appears, as shown in Figure 5-8.

4 Select Fixed Work.

Now that the task is defined by the amount of work that is performed on it, Project will adjust the task's duration and units based on this information.

Notice the "Effort driven" checkbox to the right of the "Task type" box. This option tells Microsoft Project to keep the total task work at its current value. The duration of a task shortens or lengthens as resources are added or removed from a task, while the amount of effort necessary to complete a task remains unchanged.

Since there isn't any work yet assigned to the task, don't check this box.

5 Click OK.

Table 5-2 describes how each task type works differently.

Table 5-2. Task Types

Type	Description
Fixed Duration	If a task has a fixed duration, the duration will not change. • If you revise units, Project recalculates work. • If you revise duration in a fixed-duration task, Project recalculates work. • If you revise the amount of work, Project recalculates the units.
Fixed Units	This is the default task type. If a task has fixed units, the number of assignment units will not change. • If you revise units in a fixed-unit task, Project recalculates duration. • If you revise duration, Project recalculates work. • If you revise the amount of work, Project recalculates duration.
Fixed Work	If a task has fixed work, the amount of work will remain constant. Because fixed-work tasks are effort-driven, the "Effort driven" checkbox is automatically selected for fixed-work tasks. • If you revise units, Project recalculates duration. • If you revise duration, Project recalculates units. • If you revise the amount of work in a fixed-work task, Project recalculates duration.

QUICK REFERENCE

TO DEFINE TASK TYPE:

1. SELECT THE TASK.

2. CLICK THE TASK INFORMATION BUTTON ON THE
   STANDARD TOOLBAR.

3. CLICK THE ADVANCED TAB.

4. CLICK THE TASK TYPE LIST ARROW AND SELECT
   THE TASK TYPE YOU WANT TO ASSIGN TO THE
   TASK.

5. CLICK OK.

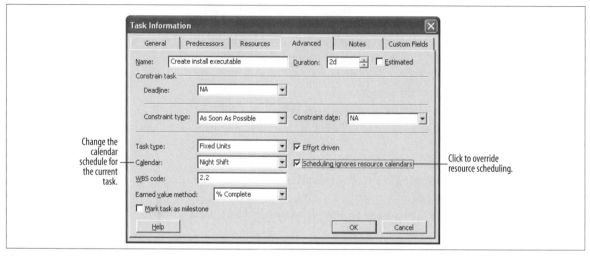

Change the
calendar
schedule for
the current
task.

Click to override
resource scheduling.

Figure 5-9. The Advanced tab of the Task Information dialog box.

By default, your tasks are scheduled according to your Project Calendar. But if a certain task needs to be done using a different calendar schedule, you can assign a different calendar to the task.

1 Select the Create install executable task.

Jeremy, the resource assigned to this task, usually works Standard hours. However, this task must be done at night while the database for the lessons is not being used.

2 Click the Task Information button and click the Advanced tab in the dialog box.

The Advanced tab appears, as shown in Figure 5-9.

3 Click the Calendar list arrow and select Night Shift from the list.

The task will now use the Night Shift calendar to schedule the working time for the task.

Notice that the "Scheduling ignores resource calendars" option is available when the task is assigned a different calendar.

4 Click the Scheduling ignores resource calendars checkbox.

This option ensures that the task calendar takes precedence over the resource calendar. This includes nonworking time scheduled for the resource.

5 Click OK.

The task changes to reflect the new schedule.

You may have noticed the empty field between the Task ID and the Task Name. This column is designated for a task indicator. A *task indicator* helps identify the task, and tells the user if there is any additional information about the task. Table 5-3 shows the task indicator icons and descriptions.

Table 5-3. Task Indicators

Icon	Description
	The task has a note attached to it.
	The task is linked to a hyperlink.
	The task has an inflexible constraint: • Finish No Later Than (for projects scheduled from the start date) • Must Start On (for all projects)
	The task has a moderately flexible constraint: • Finish No Earlier Than (for projects scheduled from the start date) • Finish No Later Than (for projects scheduled from the finish date) • Start No Earlier Than (for projects scheduled from the start date) • Start No Later Than (for projects scheduled from the finish date)
or	The task has not been scheduled or completed within the constraint's time frame.
	The task is a recurring task.
	The task is complete.
	The task is an inserted project.
	The task is an inserted project that is read-only.
	This project has already been inserted into the project or another master project.
	The task has a calendar applied to it.
	The task has nonintersecting task and resource calendars.

QUICK REFERENCE

TASK INDICATORS:

- ARE TINY ICONS THAT APPEAR NEXT TO A TASK
- HELP IDENTIFY A SPECIFIC TASK OR TASKS AT A GLANCE AND ALERT THE USER TO IMPORTANT INFORMATION

TO DISPLAY ADDITIONAL INFORMATION REGARDING A TASK:

- POINT TO THE TASK INDICATOR.

CHAPTER 6
WORKING WITH RESOURCES

CHAPTER OBJECTIVES:

Delay a resource's start time, Lesson 6.1

Change how work is distributed, Lesson 6.2

Specify resource availability, Lesson 6.3

Organize resources into groups, Lesson 6.4

Assign a new calendar to a resource, Lesson 6.5

Prerequisites

- **Have a project in which you have already entered resources.**
- **Understand project management.**

Basic resource information, such as the resource name, availability, and pay rate, is enough to successfully manage a project. However, there are many things you can do to refine a resource's schedule.

In this chapter, we'll work through some resource properties that will allow you to further define the parameters of a resource, such as applying a resource calendar and applying resource availability for different dates in the project. We'll also learn how to apply contours and delay the date a resource begins working on a task.

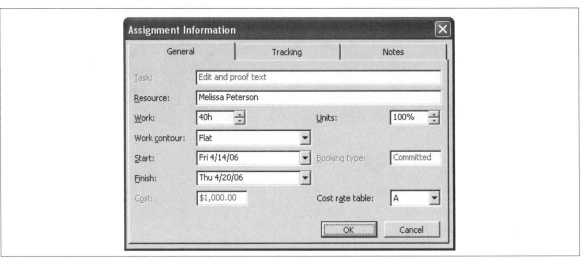

Figure 6-1. The General tab of the Assignment Information dialog box.

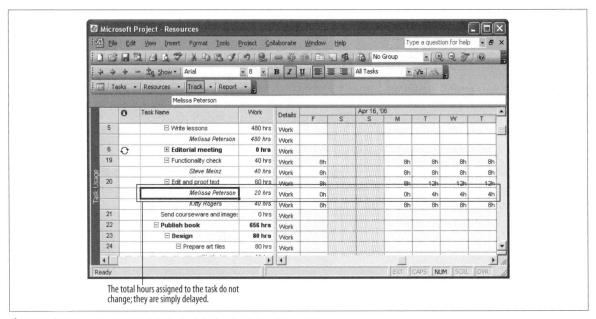

The total hours assigned to the task do not
change; they are simply delayed.

Figure 6-2. The revised rescheduled schedule for the delayed start time.

In tasks where more than one resource is assigned, you can stagger start dates of resources so they aren't all working on the task at the same time. This is useful if one resource's work has to wait until the other resources have started their work. However, spreading out work this way also extends the duration of the task. This lesson will show you how to do this.

1 Navigate to your Practice folder and open Lesson 6. Save the file as Resources.

Two resources are assigned to the "Edit and proof text" task. But one of them, the Melissa Peterson resource, doesn't have to start working on the task until later in the assignment, because she will enter the edits found by Kitty Rogers.

2 Select the Edit and proof text **task.**

To delay a resource start date, we'll use the Task Usage view.

3 Select View → Task Usage **from the menu.**

The two resources assigned to the task appear beneath the task name.

4 Select the Melissa Peterson **resource under the** "Edit and proof text" **task. Click the** Assignment Information button **on the Standard toolbar.**

The General tab of the Assignment Information dialog box appears, as shown in Figure 6-1.

Let's delay this resource so that Melissa starts working on the task two working days after the scheduled start date of the task.

5 Click the Start **list arrow and select** 4/18/06 **from the calendar menu. Click** OK.

The dialog box closes, and the resource start date has been rescheduled.

Let's take a look at how Project distributed the hours for the resource assignment.

6 Click the Go To Selected Task button **on the Standard toolbar.**

You can see the work hours scheduled for each day, as shown in Figure 6-2.

The resource works no hours on Friday and Monday, but resumes work on Tuesday. The other resource, Kitty Rogers, was not affected, but the duration of the task was. The task will now last two days longer.

QUICK REFERENCE

TO DELAY A RESOURCE START DATE:

1. SELECT THE TASK WITH THE RESOURCE YOU WANT TO DELAY.

2. SELECT VIEW → TASK USAGE FROM THE MENU.

3. SELECT THE RESOURCE YOU WANT TO DELAY.

4. CLICK THE ASSIGNMENT INFORMATION BUTTON ON THE STANDARD TOOLBAR.

5. ENTER THE NEW START DATE IN THE START BOX.

6. CLICK OK.

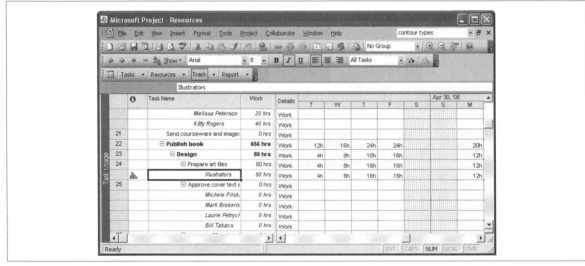

Figure 6-3. The General tab of the Assignment Information dialog box.

Figure 6-4. The resource with an Early Peak work contour.

A *predefined contour* changes how work is distributed over time. The changes a contour applies represent how the changes would look in a graphical representation. For example, the default contour is Flat—the work is distributed evenly and would not vary at all on a graph. However, a Back Loaded contour gradually increases work over a length of time.

TIP

Contours usually increase the length of a task. If you want to use a contour without increasing duration, change the task type to Fixed Duration.

First, find the task with the resource you want to change.

1 Select Edit → Go To from the menu. Type 24 in the ID text box and press Enter.

The Illustrators assigned to this task usually work fast at the beginning, and then spend less time on the task later on. Applying a work contour helps accommodate their working style.

2 Select the Illustrators resource under the "Prepare art files" task. Click the Assignment Information button on the Standard toolbar.

The General tab of the Assignment Information dialog box appears, as shown in Figure 6-3.

3 Click the Work contour list arrow and select Early Peak from the list. Click OK.

The dialog box closes, and the contour is applied to the resource, as shown in Figure 6-4. Notice that the hours scheduled for the resource start slowly at 4 hours, then rise to 16, and slowly drop back down again.

There are a number of work contours available. Table 6-1 describes each of them.

Table 6-1. Work Contours

Contour	Description
.ıll Back Loaded	Gradually increases the amount of work over time.
lı. Front Loaded	Gradually decreases the amount of work over time.
.ılıl. Double Peak	This is the most volatile contour, with two major spikes in work over the course of the task.
.ılı. Early Peak	Starts slowly, quickly increases to a high workload, and then gradually decreases to the end.
.ıll. Late Peak	Gradually increases to a high workload, and then quickly decreases at the end.
.ılı. Bell	Gradually increases, reaches a high point in the middle of the task, and then gradually decreases over time.
.ıllı. Turtle	Steady and consistent like a turtle, with slightly less work at the beginning and end of the task.

QUICK REFERENCE

TO APPLY A CONTOUR:

1. SELECT THE RESOURCE YOU WANT TO CONTOUR.

2. CLICK THE ASSIGNMENT INFORMATION BUTTON ON THE STANDARD TOOLBAR.

3. CLICK THE WORK CONTOUR LIST ARROW AND SELECT A PREDEFINED CONTOUR FROM THE LIST.

4. CLICK OK.

Specifying Resource Availability Dates

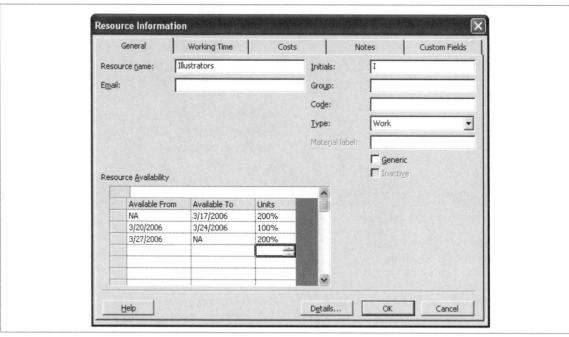

Figure 6-5. The General tab of the Resource Information dialog box.

You have already learned how to set working times for individual resources. You also entered a resource's availability in the Max. Units field when you created the resource. But you can further refine *resource availability* to specific time periods. For example, you can specify that a resource is available to work on a task 100% of the time for most of the project, but is available at only 50% for a few weeks during the project.

1 Select View → Resource Sheet from the menu.

The list of resources involved with the project appears.

2 Select the Illustrators resource.

Two illustrators are scheduled to work 100% on the project, making the total units available 200%.

3 Click the 🖹 Resource Information button on the Standard toolbar. Click the General tab.

The Resource Information dialog box appears. The Resource Availability area is at the bottom of the dialog box.

First, we have to define the availability interval for the beginning of the project in the first row. We'll leave NA in the Available From cell and enter the resource's last date of availability in the Available To cell.

4 Click the Available To cell in the first row of the Resource Availability table. Type 3/17/06 and press Enter.

This indicates that from the beginning of the project to 3/17/06, the resource is available at 200 percent.

Now enter a different level of resource availability for the time when one of the illustrators will be gone.

5 Type 3/20/06 in the Available From cell in the second row. Press Tab and type 3/24/06 in the Available To cell. Press Tab.

The interval is set, so now you just need to enter the resource availability for that time period.

6 Type 100 and press Enter.

The resource will have 100% availability from 3/20/06 to 3/24/06.

Now you have to tell Project the resource availability once the illustrator comes back to work.

7 Click the third cell in the Available From column and enter 3/27/06. Type NA in the Available To field. Press Tab.

By leaving the Available To cell as "NA", Project will assume the same resource availability until the Project's end date.

8 Type 200 in the Units cell and press Enter.

The illustrators will work with their full resource availability from 3/27/06 until the project ends, as shown in Figure 6-5.

While the Resource Availability table changes a resource's maximum units over the life of the project, it does not change resource rates over time. To set differing resource rates, set the resource cost table. But that is for another lesson…

9 Click OK.

QUICK REFERENCE

TO ENTER RESOURCE AVAILABILITY:

1. SELECT THE RESOURCE.

2. CLICK THE RESOURCE INFORMATION BUTTON ON THE STANDARD TOOLBAR.

3. ENTER THE AVAILABLE TO AND AVAILABLE FROM DATES IN THE RESOURCE AVAILABILITY TABLE.

4. ENTER THE RESOURCE AVAILABILITY IN THE UNITS FIELD.

5. CLICK OK.

Figure 6-6. The Resource Sheet sorted by groups.

Although you can't assign a group of resources to a single task, it is helpful to organize resources into logical groups for organizational purposes. Grouping allows you to view how resources are related, similar to outlining the task list.

Notice that most of the resources are assigned to a group in the Group field already. Let's assign the remaining resource to one of these groups.

1 Click the Group field for the Melissa Peterson resource.

Melissa belongs to the CustomGuide group.

2 Type CustomGuide in the Group field and press Enter.

Assigning a resource to a group is easy, isn't it?

Now let's see how the resource sheet changes when you group the resources.

3 Select Project → Group by: → Resource Group from the menu.

Your resources are now sorted into groups on your resource sheet, as shown in Figure 6-6.

Ungroup the resource and go back to viewing them in the order in which they were entered.

4 Select Project → Group by: → No Group from the menu.

QUICK REFERENCE

TO GROUP RESOURCES:

1. CLICK THE GROUP FIELD OF THE RESOURCE.

2. ENTER THE GROUP NAME.

TO VIEW RESOURCE GROUPS:

• SELECT PROJECT → GROUP BY: → RESOURCE GROUP FROM THE MENU.

Assigning a Resource Calendar

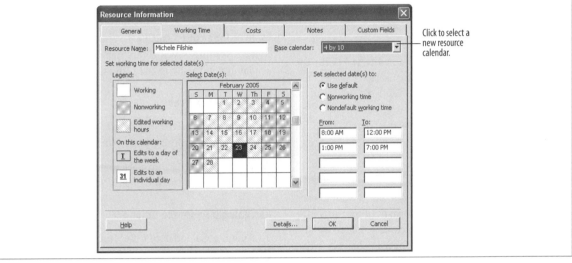

Figure 6-7. The Working Time tab of the Resource Information dialog box.

By default, your resources are scheduled according to your Project Calendar, and this book has already covered how to manage resource working time. But if a number of resources need to work from different schedules, it is easiest to just assign different calendars to these resources.

1 Select the Michele Filshie resource.

Michele will not be working Standard hours like everyone else in the project; she will be working "4 by 10": four ten-hour days per week.

This 4 by 10 base calendar has already been added to the project. Let's assign it to this resource.

2 Click the Resource Information button and click the Working Time tab in the dialog box.

This is the same tab where you can adjust nonworking time, such as vacation, for the resource.

3 Click the Base calendar list arrow and select 4 by 10 from the list.

Project will now use the 4 by 10 calendar to schedule the working time for the resource, as shown in Figure 6-7.

4 Click OK.

The resource changes to reflect the new schedule.

QUICK REFERENCE

TO ASSIGN A CALENDAR TO A RESOURCE:

1. SELECT THE TASK.

2. CLICK THE RESOURCE INFORMATION BUTTON ON THE STANDARD TOOLBAR.

3. CLICK THE WORKING TIME TAB.

4. CLICK THE BASE CALENDAR LIST ARROW AND SELECT A CALENDAR FROM THE LIST.

5. CLICK OK.

Lesson Summary

Delaying Resource Start Time

To Delay Resource Start Date: Select the task with the resource you want to delay, and then select View → Task Usage from the menu. Select the resource you want to delay and click the Assignment Information button on the Standard toolbar. Enter the new start date in the Start box and click OK when you're finished.

Applying Predefined Resource Contours

To Apply a Contour: Select the resource you want to contour and click the Assignment Information button on the Standard toolbar. Click the Work contour list arrow and select a predefined contour from the list. Click OK when you're finished.

Specifying Resource Availability Dates

To Enter Resource Availability: Select the resource and click the Resource Information button on the Standard toolbar. Enter the Available To and Available From dates in the Resource Availability table, enter the resource availability in the Units field, and then click OK.

Grouping Resources

To Group Resources: Click the Group field of the resource and enter the group name.

To View Resource Groups: Select Project → Group by: → Resource Group from the menu.

Assigning a Resource Calendar

To Assign a Calendar to a Resource: Select the task and click the Resource Information button on the Standard toolbar. Click the Working time tab, click the Base Calendar list arrow, and select a calendar from the list. Click OK when you're finished.

Quiz

1. Why would you want to delay a resource's start date? (Select all that apply.)

   A. To ensure that all resources aren't working on a task at the same time.

   B. To cut back on the duration of the task.

   C. In case one resource has to wait until another resource has started.

   D. Because you don't like them.

2. A *predefined contour* changes how work is distributed over time. (True or False?)

3. You can't refine a resource's availability once it has been entered. (True or False?)

4. You can view resource groups for a project by selecting...

   A. View → Resource Groups

   B. Project → Group by: → Resource Group

   C. Project → View → Resource Group

   D. View → Project → Grouping

5. You can't change the working calendar for just a single resource. (True or False?)

Homework

1. Start Microsoft Project 2003.

2. Navigate to your practice files and open the Homework 6 project.

3. Assign a Front Loaded contour to the "Build a chain of stands" task.

4. Your little sister is going to Girl Scout camp, so give "The Worm (little sister)" resource 50% availability from 3/24/02 to 3/31/02. (Hint: Switch to Resource Sheet view.)

5. Enter "Top employee" in the Group field for the "Snoogie" resource.

6. View the resources by Resource Group.

7. Close Homework 6 without saving changes.

Quiz Answers

1. A and C. Delaying a resource's start date *extends* the duration of the task; it doesn't cut it back.

2. True. Select from a list of predefined contours in order to change how work is distributed for a task.

3. False. You absolutely *can* refine a resource's availability for specific time periods.

4. B. View resource groups for a project by selecting Project → Group by: → Resource Group from the menu.

5. False. You can change a single resource's working calendar.

CHAPTER 7
WORKING WITH COSTS

CHAPTER OBJECTIVES:

Enter overtime rates for a resource, Lesson 7.1

Specify different pay rates for different dates, Lesson 7.2

Add pay rates for a resource, Lesson 7.3

Apply pay rates to a resource assignment, Lesson 7.4

Use consumption rates for material resources, Lesson 7.5

Enter fixed costs for a task, Lesson 7.6

Prerequisites

- **Have a project in which you have already entered tasks and their resources.**
- **Understand project management.**

Generally speaking, people and equipment generate the most expense in a project. Therefore, understanding how to fine-tune some of the costs associated with resources is a valuable skill in project management.

This chapter will show you how to specify some of the finer details in working with resource pay rates and costs. We'll also discuss other cost tasks, such as how to apply a fixed cost to a task and how to use consumption rates for material resources.

Entering Resource Overtime Rates

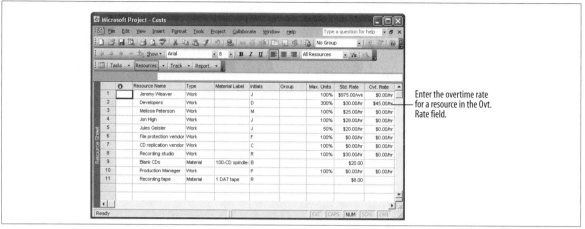

Figure 7-1. Entering an overtime rate for a resource.

Enter the overtime rate for a resource in the Ovt. Rate field.

Most resources get paid extra for working more than the standard number of hours in a regular work day or week, otherwise known as overtime. By entering an overtime pay rate, Project will automatically apply this rate for any overtime hours worked by the resource.

1 Navigate to your Practice folder and open Lesson 7. Save the file as Costs.

The Developers usually work a lot of overtime, so you'd better enter an overtime pay rate for them.

2 Click the Ovt. Rate field for the Developers resource.

Their overtime rate should be 1.5 times their standard rate.

3 Type 45 in this resource's Ovt. Rate field and press Enter.

Project will apply the overtime rate, as shown in Figure 7-1, to any overtime the resource works.

QUICK REFERENCE

TO ENTER RESOURCE OVERTIME RATES:

1. CLICK IN THE OVT. RATE FIELD OF THE RESOURCE.

2. ENTER THE RESOURCE'S OVERTIME RATE AND PRESS ENTER.

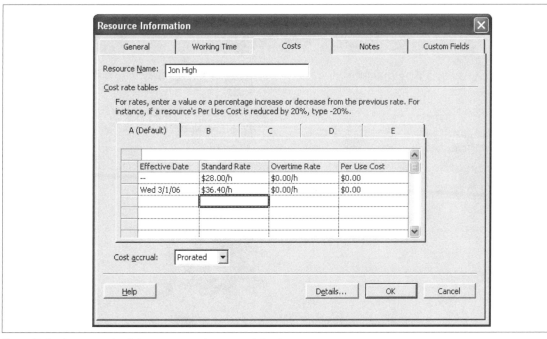

Figure 7-2. The Costs tab of the Resource Information dialog box.

Resources typically have the same pay rate for the duration of the project. However, you can apply different pay rates at different times during the project.

1 Select the Jon High resource.

This resource is due to get a significant raise (30%) during the project. Let's make Project aware of the date of the new pay rate.

2 Click the Resource Information button on the Standard toolbar.

The Resource Information dialog box appears.

3 Click the Costs tab.

The resource's default pay rate appears in the default Table A. Each tab represents a different pay rate; each resource can have up to five different pay rates.

First, enter the date the pay rate will be effective.

4 Click the second cell in the Effective Date field and type 3/1/06.

Now, enter the pay rate that will apply beginning on this date.

Instead of entering a value, you can enter a percentage in the Standard Rate field, and Project will calculate a new rate value based on the previous value.

5 Click the second cell in the Standard Rate field and type 30%. Press Enter.

The previous rate of $28 per hour plus 30% is $36.40 per hour. Compare your dialog box to Figure 7-2.

6 Click OK.

The dialog box closes. When March 1 comes around, Jon High will be paid $36.40 per hour for his work.

QUICK REFERENCE

TO SPECIFY PAY RATES FOR DIFFERENT DATES:

1. SELECT THE RESOURCE.

2. CLICK THE RESOURCE INFORMATION BUTTON ON THE STANDARD TOOLBAR.

3. CLICK THE COSTS TAB.

4. ENTER THE DATE IN THE EFFECTIVE DATE FIELD.

5. ENTER THE NEW PAY RATE IN THE STANDARD RATE FIELD.

6. ENTER OTHER COSTS (OVERTIME RATE, PER USE COST) AS NECESSARY.

7. CLICK OK.

Adding Pay Rates for a Resource

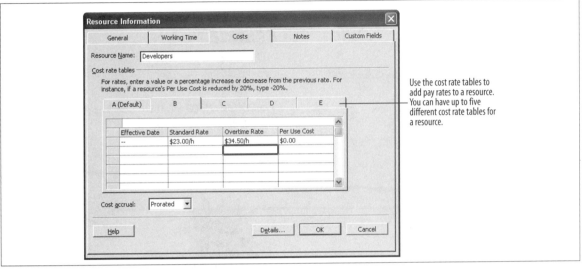

Use the cost rate tables to add pay rates to a resource. You can have up to five different cost rate tables for a resource.

Figure 7-3. The Costs tab of the Resource Information dialog box.

By default, Project uses the rates you enter when you create a resource as the pay rates for a resource. However, you can specify up to five different pay rates for a single resource. This feature is useful if a single resource requires different pay rates for different assignments.

1 Select the Developers resource.

The Developers resource is under several contracts for different pay rates in this project.

2 Click the Resource Information button on the Standard toolbar.

The Resource Information dialog box appears.

3 Click the Costs tab.

Notice that the A tab is the default pay rate. All assignments will use this pay rate by default. Let's enter a new pay rate in Table B.

4 Click the B tab.

Enter the Standard rate you want to use for this cost rate table.

5 Click the first cell in the Standard Rate column and type 23/h. Press Enter.

The new standard rate for the resource is $23 per hour.

Enter their overtime rate as well.

6 Click the first cell in the Overtime Rate column and type 34.5/h. Press Enter.

The new cost rate table is complete. Compare your dialog box to Figure 7-3.

7 Click OK.

The dialog box closes, and now the resource has two pay rates that can be applied to different assignments.

QUICK REFERENCE

TO ADD A NEW PAY RATE FOR A RESOURCE:

1. SELECT THE RESOURCE.

2. CLICK THE RESOURCE INFORMATION BUTTON ON THE STANDARD TOOLBAR.

3. CLICK THE COSTS TAB.

4. CLICK A PAY RATE TABLE TAB.

5. ENTER THE NEW PAY RATE IN THE STANDARD RATE FIELD.

6. ENTER OTHER COSTS (OVERTIME RATE, PER USE COST) AS NECESSARY.

7. CLICK OK.

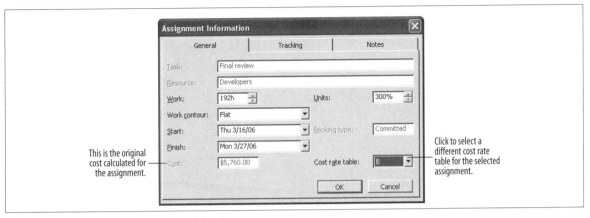

Figure 7-4. The Assignment Information dialog box.

In the previous lesson, you learned how to add pay rates to a resource. This lesson will show you how to apply one of these additional pay rates to a resource assignment.

1 Select View → Resource Usage from the menu.

The resources in the project appear.

2 Scroll down to the Developers resource.

This resource has a number of assignments. Currently, all work is being done at the same pay rate. However, the resource's contract specifies a different pay rate for the "Final review" task.

3 Select the Final Review task under the Developers resource. Click the 📄 Assignment Information button on the Standard toolbar.

The General tab of the Assignment Information dialog box appears, as shown in Figure 7-4.

The current cost calculation of the task is $5,760. This will change with a new cost rate table.

4 Click the Cost rate table list arrow and select B.

This is the pay rate table you added in the previous lesson. This pay rate is less than the original (table A), so the total cost of the assignment will drop.

5 Click OK.

The dialog box closes. Note that the calculated cost has changed: the cost with the new rate is $4,416.

QUICK REFERENCE

TO APPLY A DIFFERENT PAY RATE TO AN ASSIGNMENT:

1. SELECT VIEW → RESOURCE USAGE FROM THE MENU.
2. SELECT THE ASSIGNMENT YOU WANT TO CHANGE.
3. CLICK THE ASSIGNMENT INFORMATION BUTTON ON THE STANDARD TOOLBAR.
4. CLICK THE COST RATE TABLE LIST ARROW AND SELECT THE TABLE YOU WANT TO USE.
5. CLICK OK.

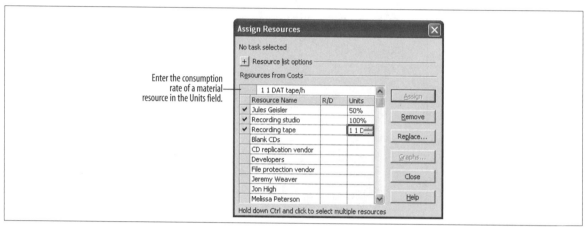

Enter the consumption rate of a material resource in the Units field.

Figure 7-5. The Assign Resources dialog box.

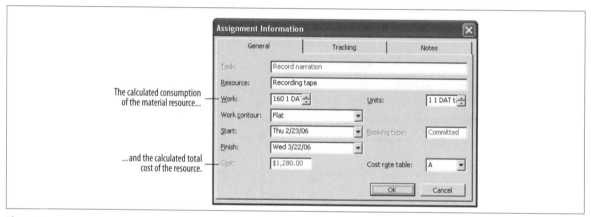

The calculated consumption of the material resource...

...and the calculated total cost of the resource.

Figure 7-6. The General tab of the Assignment Information dialog box.

In case you've forgotten, material resources are the goods needed by work resources to complete tasks. This project has one material resource: blank CDs. When you create a material resource, you enter its name, material label, and Std. Rate. But when you assign a resource to a task, you should be aware of the *consumption rate* you want to use. There are two different consumption rates:

- **Fixed consumption rate:** An absolute quantity of the resource will be used, no matter how long the task takes. For example, if you need to copy 5,000 CDs, that amount is fixed, no matter how long it takes to complete the task.

- **Variable consumption rate:** The quantity of the resource varies, depending on the duration of the task. For example, when recording narration, more recording tape is used as more narration is recorded. By using

a variable consumption rate, the calculation for the material resource will be more accurate.

In this lesson, we'll create a material resource assignment using a variable consumption rate.

1 Select View → Gantt Chart **from the menu.**

The tasks in the project appear.

2 Select the Record narration **task.**

When Jules, the resource assigned to this task, records narration, she saves the narration onto DAT recording tape.

Let's create an assignment that reflects using this material resource.

3 Click the Assign Resources button on the Standard toolbar.

The Assign Resources dialog box appears.

4 Scroll down to the Recording tape resource.

This material resource will be consumed at a variable consumption rate. Each tape is 60 minutes long, so one tape will be used per hour.

Enter this rate in the resource's Units field.

5 Click the Units field. Type 1/h and click the Assign button.

The resource is assigned to the task at a consumption rate of one DAT tape per hour, as shown in Figure 7-5.

6 Click Close.

Let's see how Project calculates this cost for the task.

7 Select View → Task Usage from the menu.

Project displays the tasks and the resources assigned to them.

8 Select the Recording tape resource. Click the Assignment Information button on the Standard toolbar.

The Assignment Information dialog box appears, as shown Figure 7-6.

QUICK REFERENCE

TO APPLY A VARIABLE CONSUMPTION RATE TO A MATERIAL RESOURCE ASSIGNMENT:

1. SELECT THE TASK TO WHICH YOU WANT TO ASSIGN THE RESOURCE.

2. CLICK THE ASSIGN RESOURCES BUTTON ON THE STANDARD TOOLBAR.

3. ENTER THE VARIABLE CONSUMPTION RATE IN THE UNITS FIELD OF THE MATERIAL RESOURCE.

4. SELECT THE MATERIAL RESOURCE AND CLICK THE ASSIGN BUTTON.

5. CLICK CLOSE.

TO VIEW MATERIAL RESOURCE COSTS:

1. SELECT VIEW → TASK USAGE FROM THE MENU.

2. SELECT THE MATERIAL RESOURCE.

3. CLICK THE ASSIGNMENT INFORMATION BUTTON ON THE STANDARD TOOLBAR.

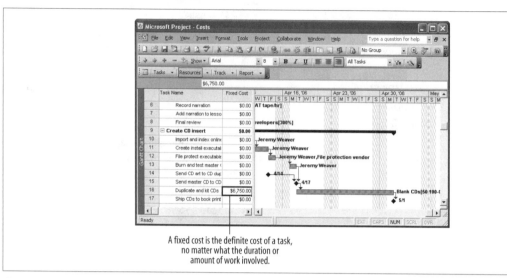

A fixed cost is the definite cost of a task, no matter what the duration or amount of work involved.

Figure 7-7. The project in Gantt Chart view with the Cost table.

Fixed costs are different from rate-based or per use costs. Fixed costs don't change if the duration or amount of work needed to complete a task changes. In this lesson, we'll assign a fixed cost to a task.

1 Select View → Gantt Chart from the menu.

The project appears in Gantt Chart view.

2 Select View → Table → Cost from the menu.

All available cost fields are displayed.

3 Select the Duplicate and kit CDs task.

The vendor for this task agreed to a one-time fee of $6,750 to complete this task.

Enter this fixed cost for the task.

4 Click the Fixed Cost field and type 6750. Press Enter.

The task is set to cost $6,750, as shown in Figure 7-7, even if the duration or amount of work changes.

TIP

If you want to enter a fixed cost for the entire project, select Tools → Options from the menu, and then click the View tab. In the "Outline options" section, click the Show project summary task checkbox, and then click OK. In the Task Name field, select the project summary task. In the Fixed Cost field, type a cost for the project.

QUICK REFERENCE

TO ENTER A FIXED COST FOR A TASK:

1. SELECT VIEW → GANTT CHART FROM THE MENU.

2. SELECT VIEW → TABLE → COST FROM THE MENU.

3. SELECT THE TASK FOR WHICH YOU WANT TO ENTER A FIXED COST.

4. TYPE THE COST IN THE FIXED COST FIELD.

Lesson Summary

Entering Resource Overtime Rates

Verify that a resource is able to work overtime before you schedule it.

To Enter Resource Overtime Rates: Click in the Ovt. Rate field of the resource you want to add overtime to. Enter the resource's overtime rate and press Enter.

Specifying Pay Rates for Different Dates

To Specify Pay Rates for Different Dates: Select the resource and click the Resource Information button on the Standard toolbar. Click the Costs tab and enter the date in the Effective Date field. Enter the new pay rate in the Standard Rate field and enter any other costs (Overtime Rate, Per Use Cost) as necessary. Click OK when you're finished.

Adding Pay Rates for a Resource

To Add a New Pay Rate for a Resource: Select the resource and click the Resource Information button on the Standard toolbar. Click the Costs tab, click a pay rate table tab, and enter the new pay rate in the Standard Rate field. Enter other costs (Overtime Rate, Per Use Cost) as necessary, and click OK when you're finished.

Applying a Different Pay Rate to an Assignment

To Apply a Different Pay Rate to an Assignment: Select View → Resource Usage from the menu, and then select the assignment you want to change. Click the Assignment Information button on the Standard toolbar. Click the Cost rate table list arrow, select the table you want to use, and then click OK.

Using Material Resource Consumption Rates

To Apply a Variable Consumption Rate to a Material Resource Assignment: Select the task you want to assign the resource to and click the Assign Resources button on the Standard toolbar. Enter the variable consumption rate in the Units field of the material resource, click the Assign button, and then click Close.

To View Material Resource Costs: Select View → Task Usage from the menu. Select the material resource and click the Assignment Information button on the Standard toolbar.

Entering Task Fixed Costs

To Enter a Fixed Cost for a Task: Select View → Gantt Chart from the menu. Select View → Table → Cost from the menu, and then select the task for which you want to enter a fixed cost. Type the cost in the Fixed Cost field.

Viewing Project Costs

To View Project Costs: Select View → More Views from the menu, select the Task Sheet view, and click Apply. Select Tools → Options from the menu and click the View tab. Click the Show Project summary task check box, click OK, and then select View → Table → Cost from the menu. Or, select Project → Project Information from the menu and click the Project Statistics button.

Quiz

1. What field should you enter resource overtime into?
   - A. The Ovt. Rate field
   - B. The Ovt. Value field
   - C. The Assigned Ovt. field
   - D. The Work Ovt. field

2. You cannot change the pay rate for different periods of the project. (True or False?)

3. You can assign up to ___ different pay rates for a single resource.
   - A. Three
   - B. Five
   - C. Four
   - D. Six

4. A *variable consumption rate* means an absolute quantity of the resource will be used, no matter how long the task takes. (True or False?)

5. A fixed cost is:

   A. a cost that has been changed to meet budget guidelines.

   B. a cost that has been assigned to an overallocated resource.

   C. a cost that has been spayed or neutered.

   D. a cost that has been assigned to a task that will not change with duration, work, or material.

Homework

1. Start Microsoft Project 2003.

2. Navigate to your practice files and open the Homework 7 project.

3. Give the Bill Gates resource an overtime rate of 150/h.

4. Give the Snoogie resource a 25% increase in pay rate on 2/18/02.

5. Go to Resource Usage view and then go back to Gantt Chart view.

6. Select the "Make a pretty sign" task and click the Assign Resources button on the Standard toolbar. You plan on making quite a few drafts, so adjust the consumption rate of the construction paper resource to 8 units per hour.

7. Give the "Buy lemons" task a fixed cost of $50.

8. Close Homework 7 without saving your changes.

Quiz Answers

1. A. Enter a resource's overtime into the Ovt. Rate field.

2. False. You can change the pay rate for different periods of the project.

3. B. You can assign up to five different pay rates for a single resource.

4. False. A *fixed consumption rate* means that an absolute quantity of the resource will be used. A *variable consumption rate* means that the quantity of the resource will vary, depending on the duration of the task.

5. D. A fixed cost does not change, even if the amount of work, materials, or duration needed to finish the task changes.

CHAPTER 8
BALANCING THE PROJECT

CHAPTER OBJECTIVES:

Schedule a resource to work overtime, Lesson 8.1

Identify overallocated resources, Lesson 8.2

Balance overallocated resources, Lessons 8.3 and 8.4

Prerequisites

- **Have a project in which you have entered tasks, resources, and costs.**
- **Understand project management.**

You may notice a few problems as you track the progress of your project; no project is perfect. For example, your project might be calculated to finish *after* your scheduled finish date. In this case, you may need to schedule some overtime work for your resources. Maybe you have some resources that are overallocated. In this case, you may need to assign work to other resources.

Most of the lessons in this chapter deal with adjusting resource work in order to balance a project's tracked progress, because resources are the easiest project element to amend. Oftentimes, problems that seem too large to handle can be easily fixed with a bit of careful resource adjustment or cost balancing. You may have touched on some of these topics in previous lessons, but use this chapter as a guide to balance your progress when problems arise in your project plan.

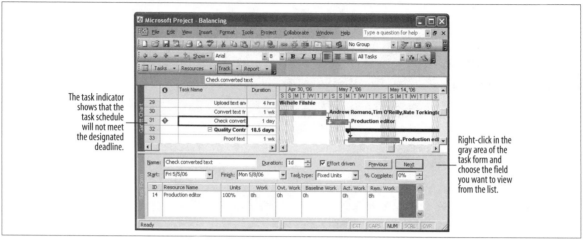

The task indicator shows that the task schedule will not meet the designated deadline.

Right-click in the gray area of the task form and choose the field you want to view from the list.

Figure 8-1. The split Gantt Chart view.

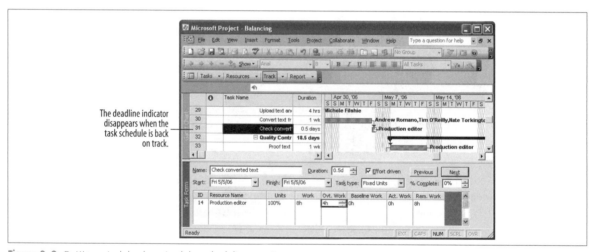

The deadline indicator disappears when the task schedule is back on track.

Figure 8-2. Putting a task back on track by scheduling overtime.

If your project schedule has slipped and tasks will not meet specified constraints, such as deadlines, you can balance this problem by scheduling resource overtime. Scheduling resource overtime means the resource can do more work on the task in a shorter amount of time. In effect, scheduling overtime reduces task duration. In this lesson, we're going to schedule resource overtime to meet a task deadline.

1 Navigate to your practice folder and open Lesson 8. Save the file as Balancing.

There is one task that, with the current schedule, won't meet its deadline.

2 Press Ctrl + G. Type 31 in the ID field and press Enter.

The Indicator field for the "Check converted text" task contains a ◆ deadline indicator, alerting you that this task won't meet its deadline.

Let's schedule some overtime so that the work required to complete this task gets done on time.

3 Select Window → Split **from the menu.**

Your window splits between a Gantt Chart screen and a Task Entry screen, as shown in Figure 8-1.

Now let's show the Work fields for the resource.

4 **Right-click in the gray area of the bottom Task Entry screen and select** Resource Work **from the short-cut menu.**

Work fields now appear in the bottom Task Entry screen. Now let's enter overtime for the resource assigned to the task, the Production editor.

5 **Click the** Ovt. Work **field for the Production editor resource in the bottom pane of the window. Type** 4h **and click** OK.

The overtime work is scheduled. Notice that there is no longer a deadline indicator for the task, and the duration of the task is shorter. Now the project plan for Task 31 is back on track. Compare your screen to Figure 8-2.

6 Select Window → Remove Split **from the menu.**

The project is displayed in the default Gantt Chart view.

QUICK REFERENCE

TO SCHEDULE OVERTIME FOR A RESOURCE:

1. SELECT THE TASK WITH THE DEADLINE INDICATOR.

2. SELECT WINDOW → SPLIT FROM THE MENU.

3. RIGHT-CLICK IN THE TASK ENTRY PANE AND SELECT RESOURCE WORK FROM THE SHORTCUT MENU.

4. CLICK THE OVT. WORK FIELD IN THE TASK ENTRY FORM.

5. ENTER THE AMOUNT OF OVERTIME YOU WANT TO SCHEDULE FOR THE RESOURCE.

6. CLICK OK.

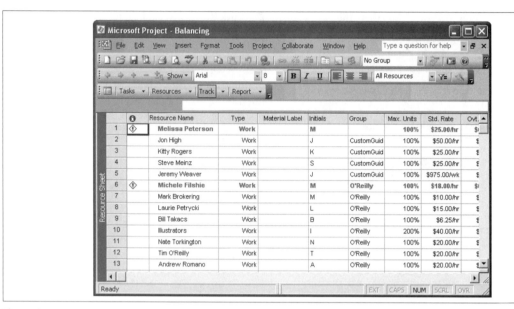

Figure 8-3. In Resource Sheet view, overallocated resources appear in red.

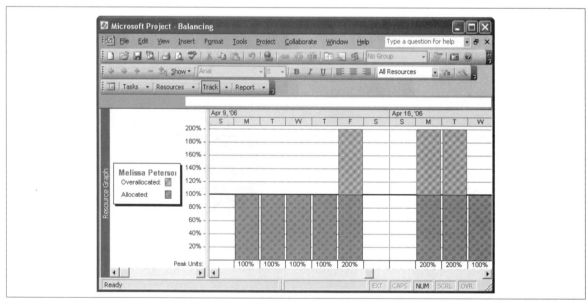

Figure 8-4. In Resource Graph view, overallocated units for the resource appear in red.

A project can be quickly thrown off balance if you have resource overallocation. *Overallocation* arises when the number of units or hours assigned to a resource are greater than the maximum number of hours available during that time period. For example, if you assigned a resource to three tasks at the same time at 100 percent, that would be an overallocated resource. It's better to recognize overallocated resources early in the project rather than after deadlines have been missed.

You can view overallocated resources in Resource Sheet view, Resource Usage view, Resource Allocation view, and Resource Graph view. In this lesson, we will balance two overallocated resources in the project.

1 Select View → Resource Sheet from the menu.

The Resource Sheet appears. The overallocated resources appear in red, as indicated in Figure 8-3.

This is probably the easiest place to spot an overallocated resource. But this view doesn't tell you where the resource is overallocated or what tasks the resource is assigned to at the time of the overallocation.

2 Select the Melissa Peterson resource. Select View → Resource Graph from the menu.

You are now in Resource Graph view.

Scroll to find the resource's overallocated dates in the graph. In this case, we'll take a shortcut and jump to the resources using the Go To dialog box.

3 Select Edit → Go To from the menu. Type 4/11/06 in the Date box. Click OK.

The dialog box closes, and the chart displays the overallocated units for the resource, as shown in Figure 8-4.

Once you identify resource overallocation, you should fix it. You can do this by using automatic leveling, by manually delaying resource work, by scheduling resource overtime (which you did in the previous lesson), or by assigning resource work to other resources.

 TIP *To change resource allocation monitoring, select* Tools → Level Resources *from the menu.*

QUICK REFERENCE

TO VIEW RESOURCE OVERALLOCATION:

1. VIEW THE PROJECT IN A RESOURCE VIEW (RESOURCE SHEET VIEW, RESOURCE USAGE VIEW, RESOURCE ALLOCATION VIEW, OR RESOURCE GRAPH VIEW).

2. FIND THE RESOURCES HIGHLIGHTED IN RED. OVERALLOCATED RESOURCES ARE ALWAYS HIGHLIGHTED IN RED.

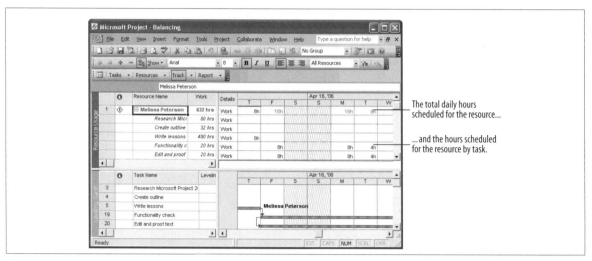

Figure 8-5. The overallocated resource in Resource Allocation view.

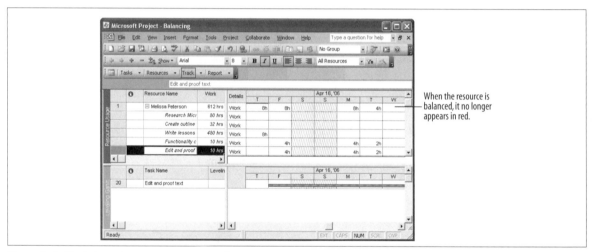

Figure 8-6. The balanced resource in Resource Allocation view.

Your resources can become overallocated when they are assigned to more work than they can finish in their scheduled working hours. Overallocated resources make your project unbalanced.

By manually balancing these overallocations, you can control how balancing affects the project. For instance, you can decide whether you want to increase the duration of a task or decrease the amount of work on the task.

1 Select View → More Views **from the menu.**

The More Views dialog box appears.

2 Select Resource Allocation **from the Views list and click** Apply.

Resource Allocation view is a split-screen view, with a timephased view on the top and a type of tracking bar chart on the bottom.

3 Select the Melissa Peterson resource and select Edit → Go To from the menu. Type 4/14/06 in the Date box and click OK.

The overallocated hours for the resource appear, as shown in Figure 8-5.

Notice that tasks are listed under their corresponding resources. If a resource does not yet have a task assigned to it, then there won't be any tasks listed underneath it.

The problem we want to fix is that the Melissa Peterson resource is scheduled to work 16-hour days on 4/14/06 and 4/17/06. This is definitely more than the resource should be required to work.

The overallocation on 4/18/06 might be confusing. Why is 8 hours of work on a single day considered an overallocation? It's because the 4 hours allocated for each task are scheduled to happen at the same time; in other words, you're cramming 8 hours of work into 4 hours of work time.

To resolve the overallocation, we'll change the resource assignment to 50% for the "Functionality check" and "Edit and proof text" tasks.

4 Click the Functionality check task under the Melissa Peterson resource.

Change the resource assignment to 50%.

5 Click the Assignment Information button on the Standard toolbar.

The Assignment Information dialog box appears.

6 Click the Units field and type 50%. Click OK.

The daily work hours are adjusted for the "Functionality check" task. However, the duration of the task is also lengthened. Rather than allowing the task to extend the duration of the project, reduce the work hours for the task.

7 Click the Smart Tag Actions button next to the resource and select the Change the tasks' total work (person-hours) to match the units and duration option.

The amount of work for the task is reduced, and the task is returned to its original duration.

Despite changing the resource's assignment, notice that the Melissa Peterson resource is still overallocated. Reduce the resource availability for the "Edit and proof text" task as well.

8 Click the Edit and proof text task under the Melissa Peterson resource.

Change the resource assignment to 50%.

9 Click the Assignment Information button on the Standard toolbar. Click the Units field and type 50%. Click OK.

Once again, the daily hours are adjusted, but the task duration is extended.

10 Click the Smart Tag Actions button next to the resource and select the Change the tasks' total work (person-hours) to match the units and duration option.

Finally, Melissa Peterson is no longer overallocated, as shown in Figure 8-6.

There are many other ways this resource could have been balanced. For example, Melissa could have been removed from one of the tasks and assigned to work on one of the tasks full time, instead of devoting part time to both of them. When resolving resource overallocation manually, you have to use your own knowledge about the project as a whole to find the best way to balance everything.

You resolved this resource overallocation manually, but you can also use a Project feature called resource leveling to resolve overallocations automatically. Move on to the next lesson to learn more about it.

QUICK REFERENCE

TO BALANCE AN OVERALLOCATED RESOURCE MANUALLY:

1. SELECT VIEW → MORE VIEWS FROM THE MENU.

2. SELECT THE RESOURCE ALLOCATION VIEW AND CLICK APPLY.

3. LOCATE THE OVERALLOCATED RESOURCE AND THE DATES AND WORK HOURS OF THE OVERALLOCATION.

4. SELECT THE TASK TO WHICH THE RESOURCE IS OVERALLOCATED.

5. CLICK THE ASSIGNMENT INFORMATION BUTTON ON THE STANDARD TOOLBAR.

6. CHANGE THE ASSIGNMENT PROPERTIES AS NECESSARY.

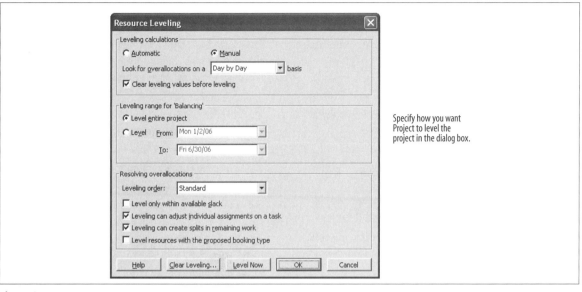

Figure 8-7. The Resource Leveling dialog box.

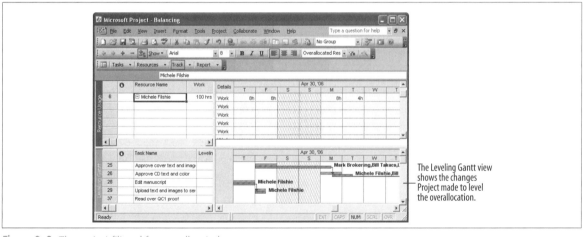

Figure 8-8. The project filtered for overallocated resources.

If you're not sure of the best way to balance an overallocated resource, you can leave it up to Project to level the resource instead. In leveling, Project splits and delays tasks in order to get rid of resource overallocation. Project tries to level only noncritical tasks (tasks with slack) to avoid affecting other tasks' schedules, because leveling often results in later start and finish dates for an overallocated task's successors.

This lesson shows you how to use leveling to balance overallocations in your project.

1 Select View → Resource Usage from the menu.

The top pane displays the project in Resource Usage view, and the bottom displays the Leveling Gantt view.

First, find the overallocated resource you want to level.

2 Select Project → Filtered for → Overallocated Resources from the menu.

The table is now filtered so that only overallocated resources appear.

3 Select the Michele Filshie resource and click the Go To Selected Task button on the Standard toolbar. Scroll to the right until you see the date 4/28/06.

Notice that Michele Filshie is scheduled to work 12 hours on April 28. Let's level the resource's workload so that she is not overallocated.

4 Select Tools → Level Resources from the menu.

The Resource Leveling dialog box appears, as shown in Figure 8-7. Here you can specify how you want leveling to occur in the project.

5 Make sure the Manual and Level entire project options are selected.

These are the default leveling options. They mean that all the resources in the project will be leveled when you click the Level Now button in the dialog box.

6 Click the Level Now button.

The Level Now dialog box appears.

7 Select the Entire pool option and click OK.

The Resource Leveling dialog box closes and the project is leveled, as shown in Figure 8-8.

How did Project level the resource? It increased the duration of the "Approve cover text and images" task to 1.5 days. You can see the changes made by Project in the chart area of the view. Green bars indicate how the tasks were scheduled before leveling; blue bars indicate the current schedule of the tasks.

QUICK REFERENCE

TO LEVEL YOUR RESOURCES AUTOMATICALLY:

1. SELECT VIEW → RESOURCE USAGE FROM THE MENU.

2. SELECT PROJECT → FILTERED FOR → OVERALLOCATED RESOURCES FROM THE MENU.

3. SELECT THE OVERALLOCATED RESOURCE(S) AND SELECT TOOLS → LEVEL RESOURCES FROM THE MENU.

4. CLICK THE MANUAL OPTION AND THE LEVEL ENTIRE PROJECT OPTION, AND THEN CLICK THE LEVEL NOW BUTTON.

5. CLICK EITHER THE SELECTED RESOURCES OPTION OR THE ENTIRE POOL OPTION, AND THEN CLICK OK.

Chapter Eight Review

Lesson Summary

To Schedule Overtime for a Resource

To Schedule Resource Overtime: Select the task that has a deadline indicator next to it and select Window → Split from the menu. Right-click in the Task Entry pane and select Resource Work from the shortcut menu. Click the Ovt. Work field in the Task Entry form and enter the amount of overtime you want to schedule for the resource. Click OK when you're finished.

Identifying Resource Overallocation

To View Resource Overallocation: View the project in a resource view and find resources highlighted in red. Overallocated resources are always highlighted in red.

Balancing Resource Overallocation Manually

To Balance Overallocation Manually: Select View → More Views from the menu, select Resource Allocation, and click Apply. Locate the overallocated resource and the dates and work hours of the overallocation. Select the task to which the resource is overallocated. Click the Assignment Information button on the Standard toolbar and change the Assignment properties as necessary.

"Delaying" a task means that you are postponing it until your assigned resource has time to work on it so the resource will not be overallocated. Some people prefer this method of fixing overallocation, while others prefer to let Project fix it automatically.

Balancing Resource Overallocation Automatically

To Automatically Level Your Resources: Select View → Resource Usage from the menu, and then select Project → Filtered For → Overallocated Resources from the menu. Select the overallocated resource(s) and select Tools → Level Resources from the menu. Click the Manual option and the Level Entire Project option, and then click the Level Now button. Click the Selected Resources option or the Entire Pool option and click OK.

"Leveling" a resource means that you allow Project to delay or split tasks so that their resources will no longer be overallocated. Some people prefer this method of fixing overallocation, and others prefer to fix overallocation manually.

When you reassign a resource to a task, you may lose your updated information for that task. For example, if the task is 30% done before you reassign a new resource to it, you will have to enter 30% again after reassignment.

Quiz

1. Overallocated resources appear in which color?

    A. Black

    B. Red

    C. Blue

    D. Chartreuse

2. What field should you enter resource overtime into?

    A. The Ovt. Rate field

    B. The Ovt. Value field

    C. The Assigned Ovt. field

    D. The Work Ovt. field

3. When it is impossible to resolve an overallocated resource, you can _____ the overallocated resource's work.

    A. just conveniently forget to do

    B. throw out

    C. reassign

    D. restructure

4. When manually delaying a task, never enter more lag (delay) time than you have slack time. (True or False?)

5. Automatic leveling allows Project to ____ and ____ tasks in order to get rid of resource overallocation.

    A. track and balance

    B. cut and paste

    C. split and delay

    D. reschedule and reassign

6. Generally, Project will only level ____ tasks (tasks with slack), to avoid affecting other tasks' schedules.

    A. unimportant

    B. noncritical

    C. superfluous

    D. underassigned

Homework

1. Start Microsoft Project 2003.

2. Navigate to your practice files and open the Homework 8 database.

3. Identify the overallocated resource.

4. Fix the overallocated resource using automatic leveling. (If you get a dialog box that says the overallocated task can't be leveled, push the Stop button and continue.)

5. Manually delay task #23, "Build a chain of stands," five days.

6. For task #5, "Build stand," give the Bill Gates resource an overtime rate of five hours. (Note that the duration of task #5 will change.)

7. Close the Homework 8 file without saving any changes.

Quiz Answers

1. B. Overallocated resources appear in red.

2. A. Enter a resource's overtime into the Ovt. Rate field.

3. C. When it is impossible to resolve an overallocated resource, you can reassign the overallocated resource's work.

4. True. If you enter more lag (delay) time than you have slack time, your schedule will be unbalanced.

5. C. Automatic leveling allows Project to split and delay tasks in order to get rid of resource overallocation.

6. B. Generally, Project will only level noncritical tasks (tasks with slack), to avoid affecting other tasks' schedules.

CHAPTER 9
UPDATING PROJECT PROGRESS

CHAPTER OBJECTIVES:

Create and save a baseline plan for your project, Lesson 9.1

Update a project's progress, Lesson 9.2

Update the actual values for a task, Lesson 9.3

Update the completion percentage for a task, Lesson 9.4

Update actual work for a task or resource, Lesson 9.5

Manually update actual costs, Lesson 9.6

Prerequisites

• **Have a project in which you have entered tasks and resources.**

• **Understand project management.**

When you're done customizing and entering tasks and resources into your project, you can sit back and ignore your project for a few weeks, right?

Wrong! Even though Project calculates your task durations, budget, etc. for you, you still need to track the progress of your project. You'll need to update your tasks, make sure resources aren't working too slow or too fast, and monitor a variety of other things. Also, tracking allows you to look up specific information, such as how much you spent on resources on a particular day. If you keep your project information up to date, you can always see the most recent status of your project, which allows you to catch problems before they get out of hand. This chapter shows you many ways to track your project.

Let's start tracking your project's progress!

Saving a Baseline Plan

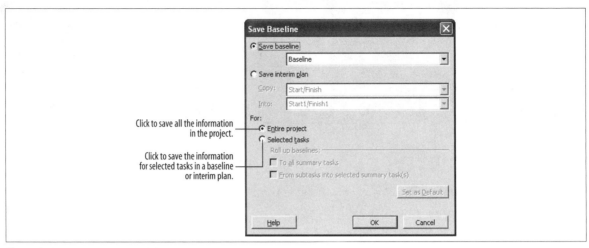

Click to save all the information in the project.

Click to save the information for selected tasks in a baseline or interim plan.

Figure 9-1. The Save Baseline dialog box.

When you have entered your best estimates for the majority of tasks, resources, and costs into your project and you're ready to start working, you should save a baseline for your project. A *baseline* is a snapshot of your project's status before work on the project begins, and is saved within the project file. For example, when you save a baseline, Microsoft Project copies the information from the Start and Finish fields into the Baseline Start and Baseline Finish fields. The baseline is the primary reference point against which you measure progress in your project.

You can modify baseline data to accommodate changes in the project, such as combining, adding, and deleting tasks. You can also remove all the data from a baseline, which you might want to do if the project is over and you want to use the project plan as a template for a future project.

*Save a baseline plan **before** you begin tracking and updating progress. That way you will have something to refer to when tracking progress changes.*

What information is included in the baseline plan?

- Tasks (start and finish dates, duration, work, cost, timephased work, and timephased cost)

- Resources (work, cost, timephased work, and timephased cost)

- Assignments (start and finish dates, work, cost, timephased work, and timephased cost)

- Baseline plan information is stored in the Baseline Start, Baseline Finish, Baseline Work, Baseline Duration, and Baseline Cost fields.

Once you start working on your project, you can use the baseline information as a reference point and see the progress that you make. For example, you want to keep track of a task's cost. The baseline estimate is $50, but the actual cost is $60, a variance of $10. Now that you know this information, you can adjust other parts of your project to meet cost constraints.

Note, however, that you can only view the variances of those items for which you've entered baseline estimates. For example, if you don't enter resource costs before you save a baseline, you will not be able to view resource-cost variances.

One more thing: always save a baseline wisely. There may be times when a project is so small that you don't need to compare progress, or you won't have enough time to check project variance. Also, if you haven't entered enough information in the file to create a baseline, simply choose to save your project without a baseline until more information is ready to go.

1 Navigate to your Practice folder and open Lesson 9. Save the file as Project Tracking.

Make sure that you save a baseline before tracking and updating project progress.

2 Select Tools → Tracking → Save Baseline from the menu.

The Save Baseline dialog box appears, as shown in Figure 9-1.

You can save up to 11 baselines for a single project.

There are two ways to save a baseline:

- **Entire project:** Choose this option if you have not saved a baseline yet for the project. This saves baseline information on all tasks in the project.

- **Selected tasks:** Choose this option to save a baseline for a specific set of tasks in the project.

We haven't saved a baseline yet, so save the entire project.

3 Make sure the Save Baseline and Entire Project options are selected. Click OK.

That's it—you have saved a baseline for your project. Now, as work is completed and tasks are updated, you can compare your work with the baseline to see how far along you are, and to see how close your planning estimates were.

⸴ NOTE ⸴ *After you save a baseline plan and begin updating your schedule, you may want to save an interim plan periodically. By comparing baseline or current information with an interim plan, you can track only task start and finish dates, not work or costs. You can save up to 10 interim plans as you work to compare levels of progress—more on those later.*

That's all there is to saving a baseline plan. The trick is to use the baseline information to track how your project is progressing, which you will learn more about as the project develops.

QUICK REFERENCE

TO SAVE A BASELINE PLAN:

1. SELECT TOOLS → TRACKING → SAVE BASELINE FROM THE MENU.

2. MAKE SURE THE SAVE BASELINE AND ENTIRE PROJECT OPTIONS ARE SELECTED.

3. CLICK OK.

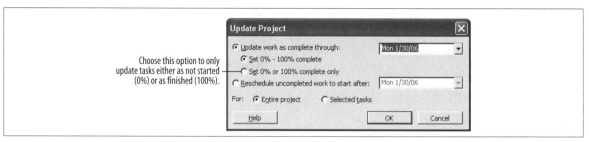

Choose this option to only
update tasks either as not started
(0%) or as finished (100%).

Figure 9-2. The Update Project dialog box.

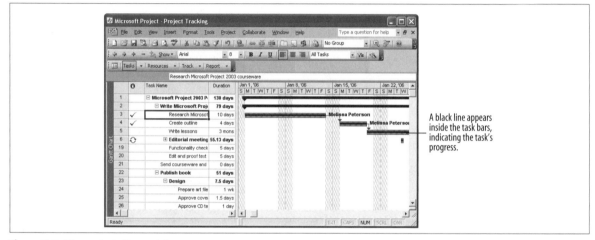

A black line appears
inside the task bars,
indicating the task's
progress.

Figure 9-3. The project after updating progress.

If everything is going along smoothly and there are no problems or delays, the easiest way to track progress is simply to report that the project is proceeding as planned. We'll hope for your sake that you will get to use this tracking method often. This lesson will show you how to do this.

In our project, the table of contents and research tasks finished on time, and the writing progress seems to be on track. Here's how to update this first month of the project.

⁝ NOTE ⁝ *Using this method of updating the project will override other tracking changes you may have made in the project.*

1 **Select** Tools → Tracking → Update Project **from the menu.**

The Update Project dialog box appears.

There are two ways to update work in the project.

• **Set 0% – 100% complete:** Updates the scheduled progress on all tasks within the given time frame.

• **Set 0% or 100% complete only:** Only updates tasks as not started (0%) or finished (100%). Does not update progress on tasks that have started but are not finished.

Let's update the project using the default options.

2 **Make sure the default options are selected, as shown in Figure 9-2.**

Now define how far into the project you want to update.

3 **Click the** Update work as complete through **list arrow.**

A calendar menu appears.

4 Navigate to and select the date 1/30/06.

Another way to enter a date is to click in the text box and type the date through which you want to update the project.

The date appears in the dialog box, as shown in Figure 9-2. Project will update the scheduled progress of tasks up to the selected date.

Once the options are selected as you want them, you're ready to update the project.

5 Click OK.

The dialog box closes, and Project updates the completion progress of tasks within the defined timeframe, as shown in Figure 9-3.

Notice that some progress has even been recorded for the "Write lessons" task, which has started but is not finished.

QUICK REFERENCE

TO UPDATE PROJECT PROGRESS:

1. SELECT TOOLS → TRACKING → UPDATE PROJECT FROM THE MENU.

2. SELECT THE OPTIONS YOU WANT TO USE TO UPDATE THE PROJECT.

3. CLICK THE UPDATE WORK AS COMPLETE THROUGH LIST ARROW AND SELECT THE DATE THROUGH WHICH YOU WANT TO UPDATE THE PROJECT.

4. CLICK OK.

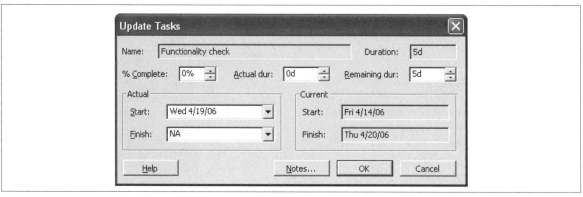

Figure 9-4. The Update Tasks dialog box.

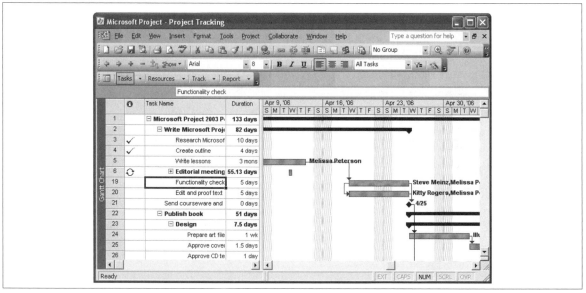

Figure 9-5. The rescheduled project after adjusting a task's actual start date.

Some tasks in your project will not fall within their scheduled time frame; some tasks may end faster or slower than scheduled. In these instances, you should update what actually happens in the project. When actual values are entered, Project adjusts the other actual values for the task and recalculates the task's completion percentage. For example, if a task started later than scheduled, entering the actual start date will cause Project to reschedule the task based on the actual date.

1 **Select the** Functionality check **task.**

This task started three days late. Update the actual start date for the task.

2 **Select** Tools → Tracking → Update Tasks **from the menu.**

 Another way to update tasks is to select View → Toolbars → Tracking *from the menu, and click the* Update Tasks button *on the Tracking toolbar.*

The Update Tasks dialog box appears.

Notice that the dialog box displays the scheduled start and finish dates in the Current area of the dialog box. These will change when you enter the actual start date.

3 Click the Start list arrow in the Actual section of the dialog box.

A calendar menu appears. If the task started three days late, accounting for the weekend, the task must start on April 19.

4 Navigate to and select the date 4/19/06.

Compare your dialog box to the one in Figure 9-4. Project will reschedule the start date of the task to the selected date.

5 Click OK.

The dialog box closes, and the task is rescheduled. Notice that the successor tasks are also rescheduled due to the change, as shown in Figure 9-5.

When possible, if the actual outcome for a task is different from the scheduled outcome, you should enter the new data in the project. Table 9-1 displays more information about how entering task actuals affects the project schedule.

⦂ NOTE ⦂ An actual duration is the amount of duration work already done, while a remaining duration is the amount of duration work left to do.

Table 9-1. Reporting Task Actuals

Actual	Rescheduling Effect
Start date	Project adjusts the task scheduled to begin on the actual start date.
Finish date	Project adjusts the task to end on the actual finish date and updates the task to 100% complete.
Actual duration	**If less than scheduled:** Project subtracts the actual duration from the scheduled duration to determine the remaining duration. **If equal to scheduled:** Project updates the task to 100% complete. **If longer than scheduled:** Project adjusts the task duration and updates the task to 100% complete.
Remaining duration	Project adds the actual duration and the remaining duration to determine the scheduled duration.

QUICK REFERENCE

TO UPDATE TASK ACTUAL VALUES:

1. SELECT THE TASK YOU WANT TO UPDATE.

2. SELECT TOOLS → TRACKING → UPDATE TASKS FROM THE MENU.

3. ENTER THE TASK ACTUAL VALUES IN THE DIALOG BOX.

4. CLICK OK.

Updating Task Completion Percentage

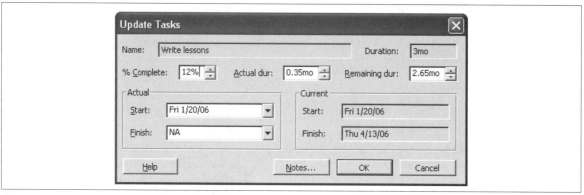

Figure 9-6. The Update Tasks dialog box.

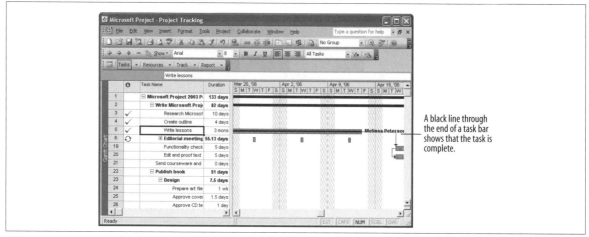

Figure 9-7. The updated task in the Gantt chart.

The quickest way to track the progress of an individual task is by recording its completion percentage. For example, it's easier to say that a mark is half done than to say that 25 of the 50 scheduled work hours have been completed. Tracking task progress allows Project to recalculate your schedule. Let's practice updating task progress by its completion percentage.

1 **Select the** Write lessons **task.**

Let's tell Project the task is 100% complete.

2 **Select** Tools → Tracking → Update Tasks **from the menu.**

The Update Tasks dialog box appears, as shown in Figure 9-6. When you enter a completion percentage for a task, Project calculates the task's actual and remaining duration using this number.

⌇ *NOTE* ⌇ *Entering a completion percentage for summary tasks updates the progress of its subtasks.*

3 **Click in the** % Complete **box. Type** 100 **and click** OK.

The task is updated to full completion, as shown in Figure 9-7.

QUICK REFERENCE

TO UPDATE TASK COMPLETION PERCENTAGE:

1. SELECT THE TASK YOU WANT TO UPDATE.

2. SELECT TOOLS → TRACKING → UPDATE TASKS FROM THE MENU.

3. CLICK THE % COMPLETE BOX AND ENTER THE COMPLETION PERCENTAGE.

4. CLICK OK.

Updating Actual Work

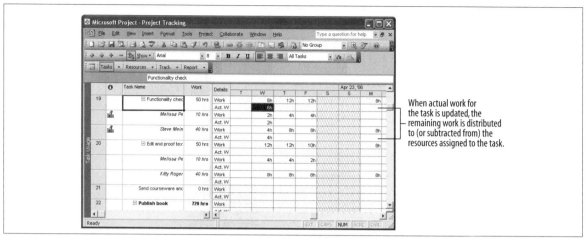

When actual work for the task is updated, the remaining work is distributed to (or subtracted from) the resources assigned to the task.

Figure 9-8. Updating actual work in Task Usage view.

If you want to be really specific about the progress of a task or resource assignment, you can record the actual work completed on a task or the amount of work done by a resource. This lesson will show you how to update the amount of actual work completed on a specific day.

1 Select View → Task Usage from the menu.

Task Usage view displays all the tasks in the project and the resources assigned to those tasks. Now, view the actual work information for the task.

2 Select Format → Details → Actual Work from the menu.

The view changes to display only the actual work done on the task.

3 Select the Functionality check task. Click the Go To Selected Task button on the Standard toolbar.

Notice that you can enter either the actual work done by an individual resource or the actual work for the task as a whole.

Let's update the actual work done toward completing the task on Wednesday, 4/19/06.

4 Click the Act. Work field for Wednesday, 4/19/06. Make sure you select the Actual Work field for the "Functionality check" task.

Now, enter the amount of work that was done on the task that day.

5 Enter 6h and press Enter.

The actual work for the "Functionality check" task has been updated. The remaining work is divided among the resources assigned to the task, and an indicator appears in the Indicators field, as shown in Figure 9-8.

When you're finished working with actual work, deselect it from the Details menu.

6 Select Format → Details → Actual Work from the menu.

The view is returned to the default Task Usage view.

QUICK REFERENCE

TO UPDATE ACTUAL WORK:

1. SELECT VIEW → TASK USAGE FROM THE MENU.

2. SELECT FORMAT → DETAILS → ACTUAL WORK FROM THE MENU.

3. CLICK THE ACT. WORK FIELD UNDER THE DATE YOU WANT TO UPDATE. MAKE SURE YOU SELECT THE ACT. WORK FIELD FOR THE TASK OR RESOURCE YOU WANT TO UPDATE.

4. ENTER THE ACTUAL AMOUNT OF WORK COMPLETED AND PRESS ENTER.

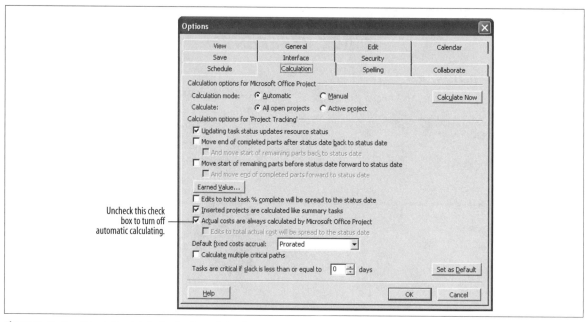

Uncheck this check box to turn off automatic calculating.

Figure 9-9. The Calculation tab in the Options dialog box.

Figure 9-10. The Act. Cost field in Task Usage view.

Even though Project automatically updates costs as tasks progress, there are times when you might want to update your costs manually, such as when the project is done and you want to enter the actual costs of tasks. Be cautious about updating costs. Once you turn the automatic updating option off, you can't turn it back on again. If you do, all the actual cost values you enter will be removed.

TIP

To update actual costs on a daily basis, select Format → Details → Costs *from the menu.*

First, turn off the automatic updating option.

1 Select Tools → Options from the menu and click the Calculation tab.

The Calculation tab of the Options dialog box appears, as shown in Figure 9-9.

2 Uncheck the Actual costs are always calculated by Microsoft Office Project checkbox, and click OK.

We're already in Task Usage view, but we need to look at the right table from this view.

3 Select View → Table → Tracking from the menu.

Update the cost for the "Write lessons" task.

4 Scroll down to the Write lessons task.

This task is completed, but as it turns out, the resource for this task worked extra hours that she didn't report. Better pay her for the extra hours she worked.

5 Press Tab until you get to the Act. Cost field.

Add another $2,000 to the cost of the task.

6 Type 14000 and press Enter.

The actual cost for the task is updated, as shown in Figure 9-10.

Turn the automatic calculation feature back on.

7 Select Tools → Options from the menu and click the Calculation tab. Check the Actual costs are always calculated by Microsoft Office Project checkbox, and click OK.

A dialog box appears, warning you that if you turn on automatic calculating again, the value you just entered will be removed.

8 Click OK.

QUICK REFERENCE

TO TURN OFF AUTOMATIC COST UPDATING:

1. SELECT TOOLS → OPTIONS FROM THE MENU AND CLICK THE CALCULATION TAB.

2. UNCHECK THE ACTUAL COSTS ARE ALWAYS CALCULATED BY MICROSOFT OFFICE PROJECT CHECKBOX, AND CLICK OK.

TO MANUALLY UPDATE ACTUAL COSTS:

1. SELECT VIEW → TASK USAGE FROM THE MENU.

2. SELECT VIEW → TABLE → TRACKING FROM THE MENU.

3. SELECT THE ACT. COST FIELD FOR THE TASK OR RESOURCE YOU WANT TO UPDATE.

4. ENTER THE ACTUAL COST AND PRESS ENTER.

Chapter Nine Review

Lesson Summary

Saving a Baseline Plan

To Save a Baseline Plan: Select Tools → Tracking → Save Baseline from the menu, make sure the Save Baseline and Entire Project options are selected, and click OK.

Updating Project Progress

To Update Project Progress: Select Tools → Tracking → Update project from the menu. Select the options you want to use to update the project, and then click the Update work as complete through list arrow and select the date through which you want to update the project. Click OK when you're finished.

Updating Task Actual Values

To Update Task Actual Values: Select the task you want to update and select Tools → Tracking → Update Tasks from the menu. Or, select View → Toolbars → Tracking from the menu and click the Update Tasks button on the Tracking toolbar. Enter the task actual values in the dialog box, and click OK when you're finished.

Updating Task Completion Percentage

To Update Task Completion Percentage: Select the task you want to update, and then select Tools → Tracking →

Update Tasks from the menu. Click the % Complete box and enter the completion percentage. Click OK when you're finished.

Updating Actual Work

To Update Actual Work: Select View → Task Usage from the menu, and then select Format Details Actual Work from the menu. Click the Act. Work field under the date you want to update. Make sure you select the Act. Work field for the task or resource you want to update. Enter the actual amount of work completed and press Enter.

Updating Actual Costs

To Turn Off Automatic Cost Updating: Select Tools → Options from the menu and click the Calculation tab. Uncheck the Actual costs are always updated by Microsoft Office Project checkbox, and click OK.

To Manually Update Actual Costs: Select View → Task Usage from the menu. Select View → Table → Tracking from the menu, and then select the Act. Cost field for the task or resource you want to update. Enter the actual cost and press Enter.

Quiz

1. Saving a baseline plan is an unimportant step in project management. (True or False?)

2. Under which menu will you find Update Tasks?
   A. Edit
   B. Tools
   C. McDonalds
   D. Format

3. When you update a task's completion percentage, a _____ appears in the task bar.
   A. black line
   B. dotted line
   C. split
   D. percentage number

Homework

1. Start Microsoft Project 2003.

2. Navigate to your practice files and open the Homework 9 project.

3. Update task 5, "Build stand," with 30% completion.

4. Give tasks #8, "Buy lemons," and #9, "Buy sugar," a new actual start date of January 30, 2003. Allow the scheduling conflict, since this will not actually change the start date of any other tasks.

5. Check the project's statistics.

6. View the project's critical path.

7. Shut off the "Actual costs are always calculated by Microsoft Project" option in the Calculation tab of the Options dialog box. Open Task Usage view. Make the table a Tracking table. For task #5, "Build stand," give the Bill Gates resource an Actual Cost of $5.00.

8. Close the Homework 9 file without saving your changes.

Quiz Answers

1. False. Saving the baseline plan is very important because it allows you to track your project's progress.

2. B. You will find Update Tasks under Tools → Tracking.

3. A. When you update a task, a black line appears in the task bar, signifying the percent of completion.

CHAPTER 10
CHECKING PROJECT PROGRESS

CHAPTER OBJECTIVES:

View project statistics, Lesson 10.1

View project costs, Lesson 10.2

View the project's critical path, Lesson 10.3

Check duration, work, and cost variance, Lessons 10.4–10.6

Identify slipped tasks, Lesson 10.7

Save an interim plan, Lesson 10.8

Prerequisites

- **Have a project in which you have entered tasks, resources, and costs.**
- **Understand project management.**

Project managers are constantly checking in with resources to find out the status of tasks and of the project overall. Project has the tools you need to update each bit of information related to a project. If you keep your project information up to date, you can always see the most recent status of your project, which allows you to catch problems before they get out of hand.

This chapter will show you how to work with updating your project.

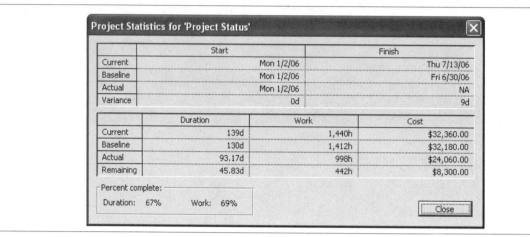

Figure 10-1. The Project Statistics dialog box.

As you work on the project, you will probably want a quick compilation of the project's statistics, such as the duration, work progress, and cost. A summary of this information appears in the Project Statistics dialog box. Here's how to find it.

1 **Navigate to your Practice folder and open** Lesson 10. **Save the file as** Project Status.

Let's view the status of a project that is just over half done.

2 **Select** Project → Project Information **from the menu.**

The Project Information dialog box appears.

3 **Click the** Statistics button.

The Project Statistics dialog box appears with the costs of the book so far, as shown in Figure 10-1.

Notice there are four types of costs in the Cost column. For descriptions of these costs, see Table 10-1.

4 **Click the** Close button.

Compare your current cost and remaining cost to see if you have enough money to finish your project as work progresses. Compare the actual cost and baseline cost to see how your project's budget is progressing.

Table 10-1. Project Statistics

Cost Type	Description
Current	The cost as it is right now.
Baseline	The project cost at the last time a baseline was saved for the project.
Actual	The cost that has been added up to the current date. For example, if a resource's pay rate is $10 an hour and it works five hours, the actual cost would be $50.
Remaining	The estimated cost that has yet to be added up.

QUICK REFERENCE

TO VIEW PROJECT STATISTICS:

1. SELECT PROJECT → PROJECT INFORMATION FROM THE MENU.

2. CLICK THE STATISTICS BUTTON.

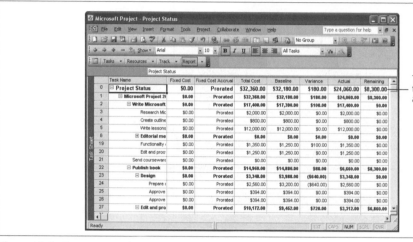

The Project summary task displays information about the entire project.

Figure 10-2. The project and project summary task costs in Task Sheet view.

The Project Statistics dialog box is useful for viewing the total costs of the project. But this lesson will show you how to view an even more detailed account of the overall costs of the project.

1 Select View → More Views **from the menu.**

The More Views dialog box appears.

2 Select the Task Sheet **view and click** Apply.

The project appears in Task Sheet view.

3 Select Tools → Options **from the menu.**

The Options dialog box appears.

You can't see it, but Project keeps a bottom-line task called the Project summary task, which is like a summary for the entire project. So to view information about the project as a whole, show the Project summary task.

4 Click the View **tab. Click the** Show Project summary task **check box and click** OK.

The summary task appears at the top of the Task Sheet.

5 Select View → Table → Cost **from the menu.**

The total costs for the project appear, as shown in Figure 10-2.

Notice that there are different fields for the original calculated cost for the project, the cost of the project up to the current date, and so on.

Hide the project summary task once again.

6 Select Tools → Options **from the menu. Click the** View **tab, click the** Show Project summary task **check-box, and click** OK.

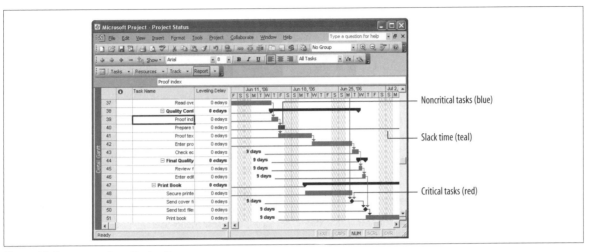

Figure 10-3. Viewing the critical path.

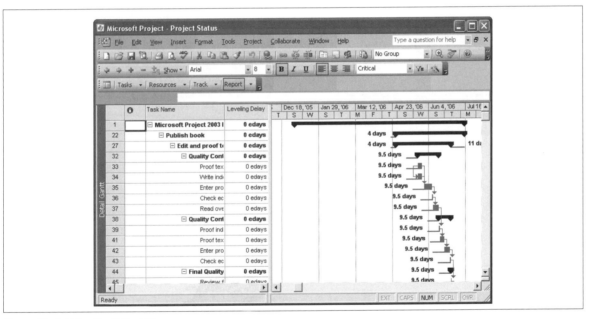

Figure 10-4. Using the Critical filter.

In a project schedule, some tasks affect the overall project length more than others do. These tasks, called *critical tasks*, must be completed on time so that the project sticks to its schedule. If a task has no slack time, it is a critical task. If a task has some slack time, it is not a critical task.

The *critical path* is the series of critical tasks that must be completed on time in order for the project to finish on schedule. Over the life of the project, the critical path will

change; if you want to shorten the duration of a project, you have to shorten its critical path. Let's take a look at this project's critical path.

1 **Select** View → More Views **from the menu.**

The More Views dialog box appears.

2 **Select** Detail Gantt **and click** Apply.

You are now in Detail Gantt view.

You may have to scroll over in the Gantt Chart to see the critical path.

3 **Press** Ctrl + G. **Type** 39 **in the ID box and press** Enter.

Notice that the task bar is red, as are some of its successor tasks. This series of linked red tasks is the critical path. Your screen should look something like Figure 10-3.

To get a better look, zoom out to view the entire project.

4 **Select** View → Zoom **from the menu. Click the** Entire Project **option and click** OK.

Now you can see critical tasks over the entire range of your project.

Scroll down through the project. Critical tasks have red task bars, and noncritical tasks have blue task bars. You should be able to see a clear representation of how the critical tasks are linked in the project.

Also, notice that many tasks have slack time on them, signified by teal lines. This means that they have until the end of the teal line to be completed without affecting the project's finish date.

Now, filter the critical path for only critical tasks.

5 **Select** Project → Filtered for: → Critical **from the menu.**

Now you can see critical tasks over the entire range of your project, as shown in Figure 10-4. Remember, as long as these tasks are on schedule, the project will stay on schedule.

Return to the Gantt Chart view.

6 **Select** View → Gantt Chart **from the menu.**

That's it! Now you just have to make sure that you and your resources stay on top of all those critical tasks.

QUICK REFERENCE

TO VIEW THE CRITICAL PATH:

1. SELECT VIEW → MORE VIEWS FROM THE MENU.
2. SELECT DETAIL GANTT FROM THE DIALOG BOX.
3. CLICK APPLY.

TO VIEW ONLY CRITICAL TASKS:

- SELECT PROJECT → FILTERED FOR: → CRITICAL FROM THE MENU.

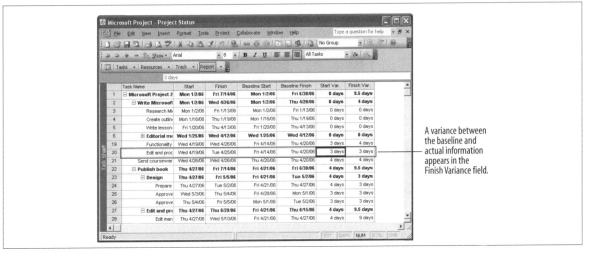

A variance between the baseline and actual information appears in the Finish Variance field.

Figure 10-5. Viewing duration variance in Task Sheet view.

Variance is the difference between baseline information and actual information in a field. Project lists variance as either positive or negative. Negative variance indicates that tasks are ahead of schedule, and positive variance indicates that tasks are behind schedule. Negative and positive variance in resource assignments can be good or bad. For instance, although it's nice when resources finish a task ahead of time, it may also indicate that your resources have not been allocated properly.

1 Select View → More Views **from the menu. Select** Task Sheet **from the dialog box and click** Apply**.**

Now you can see more task fields on one screen.

2 Select View → Table → Variance **from the menu.**

You are now in a Task Variance table view.

3 Press Ctrl + G. **Type** 20 **in the ID box and press** Enter**.**

Remember that the baseline values are the values you estimated when you planned the project. Compare the Start and Baseline Start fields to see if there is variance.

4 Look at the Start **and** Baseline Start **fields for the** Edit and proof text **task.**

The Start and Baseline Start fields have different dates in them, indicating that there is variance.

5 Look at the Start Var. **and** Finish Var. **fields for the task, as shown in Figure 10-5.**

There is a positive variance of 3 days in both the Start Var. field and the Finish Var. field, which means the task started late but took the estimated amount of time to complete.

QUICK REFERENCE

TO CHECK DURATION VARIANCE:

1. SELECT VIEW → MORE VIEWS FROM THE MENU, SELECT TASK SHEET AND CLICK APPLY.

2. SELECT VIEW → TABLE → VARIANCE FROM THE MENU.

3. VIEW THE TASK START AND FINISH VARIATIONS IN THE START VAR. AND FINISH VAR. FIELDS.

	Resource Name	% Comp.	Work	Overtime	Baseline	Variance	Actual	Remaining
1	Melissa Peterson	100%	612 hrs	0 hrs	612 hrs	0 hrs	612 hrs	0 hrs
2	Jon High	0%	0 hrs	0 hrs	0 hrs	0 hrs	0 hrs	0 hrs
3	Kitty Rogers	100%	40 hrs	0 hrs	40 hrs	0 hrs	40 hrs	0 hrs
4	Steve Meinz	100%	44 hrs	0 hrs	40 hrs	4 hrs	44 hrs	0 hrs
5	Michele Filshie	71%	140 hrs	0 hrs	100 hrs	40 hrs	100 hrs	40 hrs
6	Mark Brokering	100%	16 hrs	0 hrs	16 hrs	0 hrs	16 hrs	0 hrs
7	Laurie Petrycki	100%	16 hrs	0 hrs	16 hrs	0 hrs	16 hrs	0 hrs
8	Bill Takacs	100%	16 hrs	0 hrs	16 hrs	0 hrs	16 hrs	0 hrs
9	Illustrators	100%	64 hrs	0 hrs	80 hrs	-16 hrs	64 hrs	0 hrs
10	Nate Torkington	100%	40 hrs	0 hrs	40 hrs	0 hrs	40 hrs	0 hrs
11	Tim O'Reilly	100%	40 hrs	0 hrs	40 hrs	0 hrs	40 hrs	0 hrs
12	Andrew Romano	100%	40 hrs	0 hrs	40 hrs	0 hrs	40 hrs	0 hrs
13	Production editor	3%	188 hrs	0 hrs	188 hrs	0 hrs	6 hrs	182 hrs
14	Indexer	0%	48 hrs	0 hrs	48 hrs	0 hrs	0 hrs	48 hrs
15	Production manager	0%	56 hrs	0 hrs	56 hrs	0 hrs	0 hrs	56 hrs
16	Printer	0%	80 hrs	0 hrs	80 hrs	0 hrs	0 hrs	80 hrs

Compare a resource's work information to view its work variance.

Figure 10-6. Viewing work variance in Resource Sheet view.

You can check how much total work a resource is accomplishing by looking at the variance between a resource's baseline work and actual work. This is especially helpful if you schedule tasks based on the availability of resources. If you're managing resource assignments in your project, you need to make sure resources complete task work in the time scheduled. Since you've saved a baseline for your project, you can check the resource task work variance information.

1 Select View → Resource Sheet from the menu.

You are now in Resource Sheet view. Let's change the table to view work.

2 Select View → Table → Work from the menu.

The values in the Variance field show the difference between the current work scheduled and the amount of work originally planned, which is saved in the baseline.

3 Look at the Work and Baseline fields for the Illustrators resource, as shown in Figure 10-6.

The Work and Baseline fields have different amounts of work in them. That means there is variance. It is a negative variance of 16 hours, meaning that the Illustrators finished their task sooner than planned.

NOTE *If several # signs appear in your Baseline field, don't panic! This just means that the cell is not large enough to fit every character. In the title bar, simply drag the field's right border to the right until every character is visible.*

QUICK REFERENCE

TO CHECK RESOURCE WORK VARIANCE:

1. SELECT VIEW → RESOURCE SHEET FROM THE MENU.

2. SELECT VIEW → TABLE → WORK FROM THE MENU.

3. CHECK THE VARIANCE FIELD TO VIEW VARIANCE IN THE RESOURCE WORK.

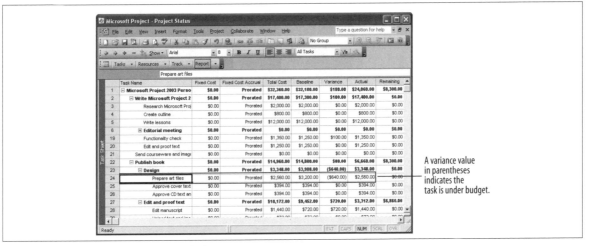

Figure 10-7. Viewing cost variance in Task Sheet view.

By checking cost variance, you can see if there are any tasks that cost more than you budgeted. You can then catch cost overruns before they become serious and adjust your schedule or budget accordingly. Project calculates the cost of each resource's work, the total cost for each task and resource, and the total project cost.

1 Select View → More Views from the menu. Select Task Sheet from the dialog box and click Apply.

Now you can see more task fields on one screen.

2 Select View → Table → Cost from the menu.

Now let's compare the values in the Total Cost and Baseline fields. Is there any variance between the fields?

3 Look at the Total Cost and Baseline fields for the Prepare art files task, as shown in Figure 10-7.

There is a variance of $640 between these fields. Notice that the value in the Variance field is in parentheses, which means that the total cost is under the baseline estimate.

⚡ NOTE ⚡ One more thing—if you want to see cost variance information for the project rolled up into one task, display the project summary task. Go to Tools → Options → View tab. Under Outline options, check the Show project summary task checkbox and click OK.

QUICK REFERENCE

TO CHECK COST VARIANCE:

1. SELECT VIEW → TASK SHEET FROM THE MENU.

2. SELECT VIEW → TABLE → COST FROM THE MENU.

3. CHECK THE VARIANCE FIELD TO VIEW VARIANCE IN THE COST.

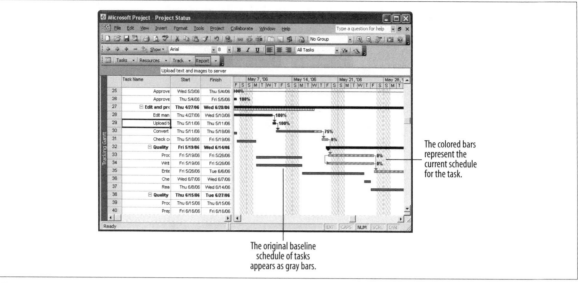

The colored bars represent the current schedule for the task.

The original baseline schedule of tasks appears as gray bars.

Figure 10-8. Slipped tasks in Tracking Gantt view.

If you don't like using Project's sheets and tables to find variance in your tasks, use Tracking Gantt view instead. It shows the current schedule on top of the baseline schedule for each task. Spots where these task bars don't line up indicate slipped tasks.

TIP

It is helpful to use the Tracking Gantt after you have begun to update progress in your project.

1 Select View → Tracking Gantt **from the menu.**

The project appears in Tracking Gantt view. Notice how current schedule work (blue) and original schedule work (black) are paired for each task. If part of the task bar is red, that means the task is critical, and the project's end date depends on that task being completed on time.

2 Select View → Table → Variance **from the menu.**

You know it's a slipped task when the top and bottom colored halves of a task bar don't line up perfectly.

3 Press Ctrl + G. **Type** 29 **in the ID box and press** Enter**.**

Your screen should look similar to Figure 10-8. At this point, the task has slipped so much that the baseline schedule isn't even close to the current schedule of tasks. Its top and bottom halves don't match up, and it is throwing off the rest of the tasks ahead of it on the timeline.

QUICK REFERENCE

TO IDENTIFY SLIPPED TASKS:

1. SELECT VIEW → TRACKING GANTT FROM THE MENU.

2. SELECT VIEW → TABLE → VARIANCE FROM THE MENU.

3. A SLIPPED TASK IS A TASK WHERE THE BASELINE AND CURRENT TASK BARS ARE NOT ALIGNED.

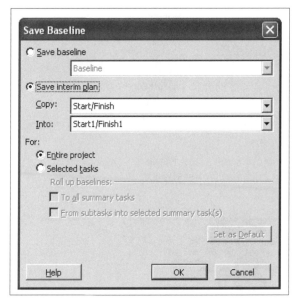

Figure 10-9. Saving an interim plan in the Save Baseline dialog box.

While a baseline plan records how the entire project looks before any progress is recorded, an interim plan is a snapshot of your project as it progresses. You can then compare interim plan data to baseline plan data to assess task progress.

Interim plans are not nearly as detailed as baseline plans. A baseline saves 20 pieces of information, whereas an interim plan saves only two pieces of information: the start and finish date of a task. You can save up to 10 interim plans at a time.

Although you generally would save an interim plan only after beginning task work, let's save an interim plan right now just for practice.

1 **Select** Tools → Tracking → Save Baseline **from the menu.**

You are going to save an interim plan, so…

2 **Click the** Save interim plan **option.**

Notice that the Copy and Into boxes are no longer shaded. When saving an interim plan, you must select values for both the Copy and Into fields.

- **Copy:** Specifies the fields you want to use to *create* the interim plan. For example, if you want to create an interim plan using the information in your baseline plan, select Baseline Start/Finish.

- **Into:** Specifies the fields that you want to use to *store* the interim plan; in other words, the plan name.

Now, select the name of the current plan and select a name for the new interim plan.

3 **Click the** Copy **list arrow.**

Notice that there are 10 options from which to choose, one for each plan you can save.

4 **Select** Start/Finish **from the list.**

The information in the Start and Finish fields will be recorded in the interim plan.

Now choose where you want to store this information.

5 **Click the** Into **list arrow and select** Start1/Finish1.

The interim plan information will be stored under this plan name.

You can either choose "Entire project" to save an interim plan for the whole project, or choose "Select tasks" to save a portion of the project. Choose to save the entire project, as shown in Figure 10-9.

6 **Click the** Entire project **option and click** OK.

After saving an interim plan, you can view the plan's start and finish dates by inserting its fields into the task sheet. For example, if you've saved three interim plans, you can view the dates saved in the third plan by inserting the Start3 and Finish3 fields into Task Sheet view.

QUICK REFERENCE

TO SAVE AN INTERIM PLAN:

1. SELECT TOOLS → TRACKING → SAVE BASELINE FROM THE MENU.

2. CLICK THE SAVE INTERIM PLAN OPTION.

3. CLICK THE COPY LIST ARROW AND SELECT THE NAME OF THE CURRENT INTERIM PLAN.

4. CLICK THE INTO LIST ARROW AND SELECT THE NAME FOR THE NEXT INTERIM PLAN.

5. CLICK THE ENTIRE PROJECT OPTION AND CLICK OK.

   OR...

   CLICK SELECTED TASKS TO SAVE A PORTION OF THE PROJECT SCHEDULE.

Chapter Ten Review

Lesson Summary

Viewing Project Statistics

To View Project Statistics: Select Project → Project Information from the menu and click the Statistics button.

Viewing Project Costs

To View Project Costs: Select View → More Views from the menu, select Task Sheet view, and click Apply. Select Tools → Options from the menu and click the View tab. Click the Show Project summary task checkbox and click OK. Select View → Table → Cost from the menu.

Viewing the Project's Critical Path

To View the Critical Path: Select View → More Views from the menu, select Detail Gantt, and click Apply.

To View Only Critical Tasks: Select Project → Filtered for: → Critical from the menu.

Checking Duration Variance

To Check Duration Variance: Select View → More Views from the menu, select Task Sheet, and click Apply. Select View → Table → Variance from the menu, and then look at the Start Var. and Finish Var. fields to see the amounts of variance calculated for the start and finish of the task.

Checking Work Variance

To Check Resource Work Variance: Select View → Resource Sheet from the menu, and then select View → Table → Work from the menu. Check the Variance field to view variance in the resource work.

Checking Cost Variance

To Check Cost Variance: Select View → Task Sheet from the menu, and then select View → Table → Cost from the menu. Check the Variance field to view variance in cost.

Identifying Slipped Tasks

To Fix Project Trouble Spots: Select View → Tracking Gantt from the menu, and then select View → Table → Variance from the menu. A slipped task is a task where the baseline and current task bars do not align with one another.

Saving an Interim Plan

To Save an Interim Plan: Select Tools → Tracking → Save Baseline from the menu and click the Save interim plan option. Click the Copy list arrow and select the name of the current interim plan. Click the Into list arrow and select the name for the next interim plan. Click the Entire project option and click OK, or click Selected Tasks to save a portion of the schedule.

Quiz

1. Actual cost is the project cost as it is right now. (True or False?)

2. Tasks that affect the overall project length more than other tasks do are called what?
   A. Subtasks
   B. Major tasks
   C. Critical tasks
   D. All tasks affect the project equally

3. Variance is the difference between baseline information and actual information in a field. (True or False?)

4. Project displays variance as _____.
   A. scrambled or sunny-side-up
   B. dangerous or safe
   C. daily or weekly
   D. positive or negative

5. By checking cost variance, you can (select all that apply):

   A. see if there are any tasks that cost more than you budgeted for.

   B. catch cost overruns before they become serious.

   C. check how much total work a resource is accomplishing.

   D. identify resource overallocation.

6. In order to identify any slipped tasks, you must be in _____ view.

   A. Gantt Chart

   B. Tracking Gantt

   C. Task Form

   D. Resource Sheet

7. An interim plan records how the entire project looks before any progress is recorded. (True or False?)

8. An interim plan saves what two types of information?

   A. The start and finish date of a task

   B. Positive and negative values

   C. Critical and noncritical tasks

   D. Simple and complicated equations

Homework

1. Start Microsoft Project 2003.

2. Navigate to your practice files and open the Homework 10 project.

3. Check the project's statistics.

4. View the costs of the project as a whole.

5. View this project's critical path, and then go back to the default view.

6. Open the Variance table in Gantt Chart view, and then find the summary task with negative variance.

7. Now, change the table from Variance to Work and find which task has work variance.

8. Close the Homework 10 file without saving any changes.

Quiz Answers

1. False. Actual cost is the cost that has been added up to the current date.

2. C. Critical tasks affect the project more than other tasks do.

3. True. Variance is the difference between baseline information and actual information in a field.

4. D. Project displays variance as positive or negative.

5. A and B. By checking cost variance, you can see if there are any tasks that cost more than you budgeted. You can catch cost overruns before they become serious and adjust your schedule or budget accordingly.

6. B. You must be in Tracking Gantt view in order to identify slipped tasks.

7. False. An interim plan is a snapshot of your project as it progresses.

8. A. An interim plan saves two pieces of information: the start date and finish date of a task.

CHAPTER 11

WORKING WITH REPORTS

CHAPTER OBJECTIVES:

Select a report, Lesson 11.1

Add page elements to a report, Lesson 11.2

Sort a report, Lesson 11.3

Define report contents, Lesson 11.4

Save a project as a web page, Lesson 11.5

Prerequisites

- **Have a project in which you have entered tasks, resources, and costs.**
- **Understand project management.**

It is important that the people who have an interest in the project understand how the project is progressing. Project's reports do just that: compile the information you need about the project in a clear, easy-to-read form. You can format, customize, define, and sort specific information in reports so they are tailored to people with specific interests. Reports are also a great way to analyze information about your project in a larger space than your computer screen.

Opening a Report

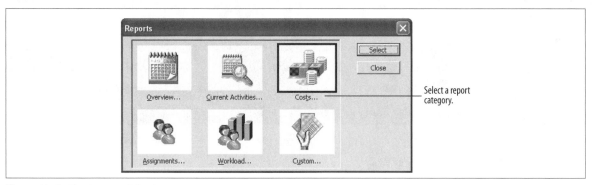

Select a report category.

Figure 11-1. The Reports dialog box.

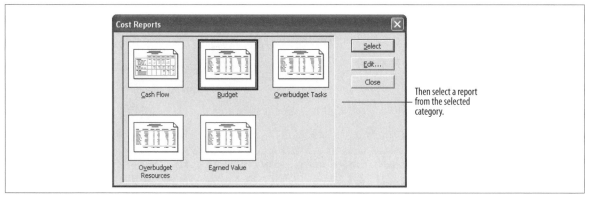

Then select a report from the selected category.

Figure 11-2. The reports grouped in the Cost category.

Reports are useful for communicating project information with others, analyzing potential problem areas in the project, and for basic project management. Microsoft Project comes with over 20 different reports, each one designed to compile a specific set of information. When a report is compiled, the information is drawn from specific fields in the project so that the report's data is always up to date and effective.

The best way to learn about reports is to just open them up and find out what they tell you. Let's try it.

1 Navigate to your practice folder and open Lesson 11. Save the file as Reports.

First, let's preview the list of Project's 22 standard reports.

2 Select View → Reports from the menu.

The Reports dialog box appears, as shown in Figure 11-1. The Reports dialog box presents you with

five different report category buttons, plus a button for creating your own custom report.

The Budget report under the "Costs" category seems to be the report we want to print, since it meets our criteria of having task, cost, and cost variance information. So, let's go find it.

3 Click the Costs category, and then click Select.

The Cost Reports dialog box appears, as shown in Figure 11-2.

4 Click the Budget report, and then click Select.

The Budget report opens in Print Preview.

Opening a report is easy; the hard part is deciding which report you want to use. The five available report categories are highlighted in Table 11-1.

Table 11-1. Report Types

Category	Reports
Overview	**Project Summary:** Shows project-level information about dates, durations, costs, task status, and resource status.
	Top-Level Tasks: Displays the scheduled start/finish dates, % complete, cost, and remaining work for summary tasks.
	Critical Tasks: Displays the planned duration, start/finish dates, resources, predecessors, and successors of critical tasks.
	Milestones: Displays the planned duration, start/finish dates, and predecessors for each milestone and zero-duration task.
	Working Days: Shows information from the project calendar.
Current Activities	**Unstarted Tasks:** Sorts by date the duration, predecessor, and resource information for each task that has not been started.
	Tasks Starting Soon: Begins with two active filters; enter a date range for use in determining which tasks are starting soon.
	Tasks In Progress: Lists duration, start and planned finish dates, and resource information for tasks that have started but aren't complete.
	Completed Tasks: Lists actual information for tasks that are 100% complete.
	Should Have Started Tasks: Shows variance information for tasks that should have started by a certain date but haven't been started/updated.
	Slipping Tasks: Shows tasks that are rescheduled from their originally planned baseline dates.
Costs	**Cash Flow:** Displays weekly costs by task.
	Budget: Lists tasks with cost and cost variance information.
	Overbudget Tasks: Shows information for tasks exceeding their baseline (originally planned) budget amounts.
	Overbudget Resources: Shows information for resources whose cost is predicted to exceed the baseline (originally planned) cost.
	Earned Value: Displays task progress in terms of dollars earned.
Assignments	**Who Does What:** Lists each resource with task assignments and information.
	Who Does What When: Lists each resource with task assignments and information on a daily basis.
	To-Do List: Shows assignments of a specific resource on a weekly basis.
	Overallocated Resources: Lists overallocated resources and their assigned task information.
Workload	**Task Usage:** Shows each task with resources and assignment information.
	Resource Usage: Shows each resource with task assignments.

QUICK REFERENCE

TO CHOOSE A REPORT TYPE:

1. SELECT VIEW → REPORTS FROM THE MENU.

2. SELECT A REPORT CATEGORY AND CLICK SELECT.

3. SELECT A REPORT AND CLICK SELECT.

Adding Page Elements to a Report

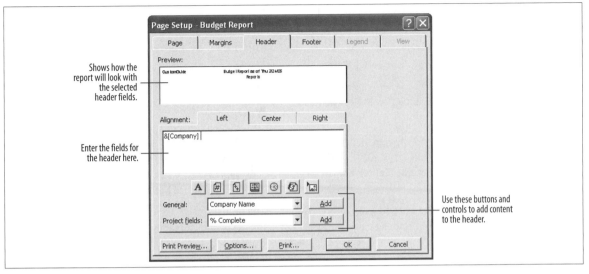

Shows how the report will look with the selected header fields.

Enter the fields for the header here.

Use these buttons and controls to add content to the header.

Figure 11-3. The Header tab of the Page Setup dialog box.

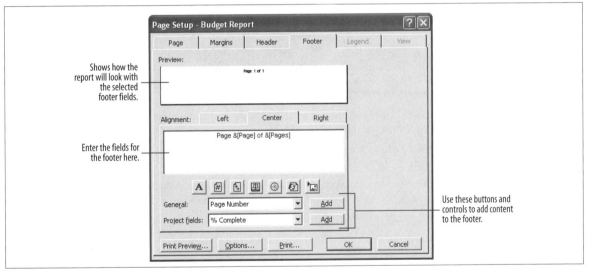

Shows how the report will look with the selected footer fields.

Enter the fields for the footer here.

Use these buttons and controls to add content to the footer.

Figure 11-4. The Footer tab of the Page Setup dialog box.

You may want to personalize your report by adding or changing a page element, such as a header, footer, margin, or border. Page elements allow you to insert your name, the project finish date, a design, and more on each page of your report. Let's add a few basic page elements to the Budget report.

1 Click the Page Setup button **on the toolbar.**

The Page tab of the Page Setup dialog box appears.

You can work with a different element of the page under each tab in the dialog box. Let's add something to the header of this report.

2 Click the Header **tab.**

The current header displays information for the type of report being used, the current date, and the project manager in the center of the header.

Let's add the company name to the left side of the header.

3 Click the Left tab in the Alignment section.

Currently, the left side of the header is empty.

4 Click the General list arrow and select Company Name from the list. Click Add.

The Company Name field is added to the header, as shown in Figure 11-3.

Now, add something to the page footer.

5 Click the Footer tab. Click the Center tab in the Alignment section.

The current footer shows the current page number. Let's add a field for the total number of pages in the report.

6 Click after the [Page] field. Type of and click the ⊞ Insert Total Page Count button in the dialog box.

The [Pages] field is added to the footer, as shown in Figure 11-4.

Now see how the changes look in the actual report.

7 Click OK.

The dialog box closes, and the header and footer changes appear in the report.

8 Click the Close button.

The report closes. The changes you made are saved for the next time you view the project in that report.

We didn't get to all the tabs in the Page Setup dialog box, but the other tabs are also very useful in formatting your project report. See Table 11-2 to find out what each tab is used for.

Table 11-2. Page Setup Tabs

Tab	Description
Page	This tab doesn't allow you to add page elements, but it does allow you to change the scope of your page. The options in this tab are self-explanatory.
Margins	Using this tab, you can adjust any margin setting using the up and down arrow buttons, and you can choose whether or not you want a border on your pages.
Header	This tab allows you to add text or a picture at the top of your printed pages. You can align text in a header to the left, center, or right by clicking on the corresponding tab.
Footer	This tab allows you to add text or a picture at the bottom of your printed pages. You can align text in a footer to the left, center, or right by clicking on the corresponding tab.
Legend	This tab is accessible only when you add page elements to printed views.
View	This tab is accessible only when you add page elements to printed views.

QUICK REFERENCE

TO ADD PAGE ELEMENTS TO A REPORT:

1. OPEN A REPORT.

2. IN PRINT PREVIEW, CLICK THE PAGE SETUP BUTTON.

3. IN THE PAGE SETUP DIALOG BOX, USE THE VARIOUS TABS TO ADD PAGE ELEMENTS TO YOUR REPORT.

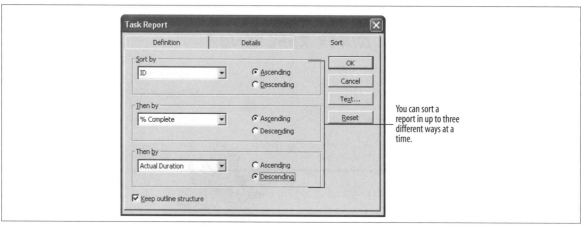

Figure 11-5. The Sort tab of the Task Report dialog box.

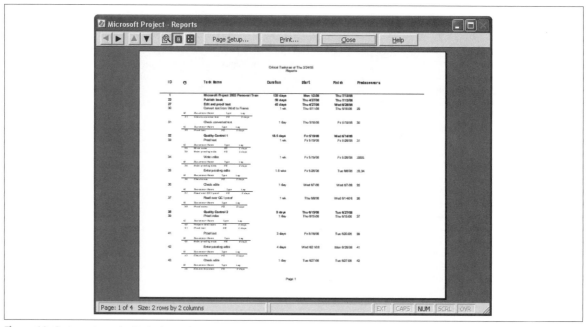

Figure 11-6. A preview of a Project report.

Sorting a report allows you to put your report information in a certain order. You can't sort all of Project's standard reports, but many reports have a variety of sort options, such as by task ID, duration, or resource initials.

1 Select the Overview report category and click Select.

The Overview Reports dialog box appears.

2 Select the Critical Tasks report and click the Edit button.

The Task Report dialog box appears.

You want to sort report contents, so…

3 Click the Sort tab.

This is where you can choose how you want to sort your report.

Let's sort the report by ID in ascending order, then by % Complete in ascending order, and finally by Actual Duration in descending order.

4 Click the Sort by list arrow and select ID from the list. Make sure the Ascending option is selected.

The report will be sorted by ID in ascending order.

5 Click the first Then by list arrow and select % Complete from the list. Make sure the Ascending option is selected.

After sorting by ID, the report will sort by the task's completion percentage in ascending order.

6 Click the second Then by list arrow and select Actual Duration from the list. Click the Descending option.

Compare your sorting options to Figure 11-5.

Now that you have chosen your sorting options, you are ready to preview your report to see the sort.

7 Click OK.

You are back to the Overview Reports dialog box. Now let's preview the report.

8 Make sure the Critical Tasks report is selected, and then click Select.

The sorted Critical Tasks report appears in Print Preview, as shown in Figure 11-6.

9 Click the Close button to close the report.

QUICK REFERENCE

TO SORT A REPORT:

1. SELECT A REPORT AND CLICK THE EDIT BUTTON.

2. IF THE REPORT IS SORTABLE, THE TASK REPORTS DIALOG BOX WILL APPEAR. (NOT ALL REPORTS ARE SORTABLE.)

3. CLICK THE SORT TAB.

4. SELECT YOUR SORTING OPTIONS.

5. CLICK OK.

6. CLICK THE SELECT BUTTON TO PREVIEW YOUR SORTED REPORT.

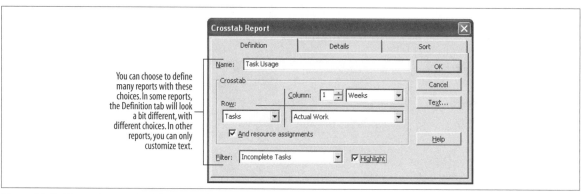

You can choose to define many reports with these choices. In some reports, the Definition tab will look a bit different, with different choices. In other reports, you can only customize text.

Figure 11-7. The Definition tab of the Crosstab Report dialog box.

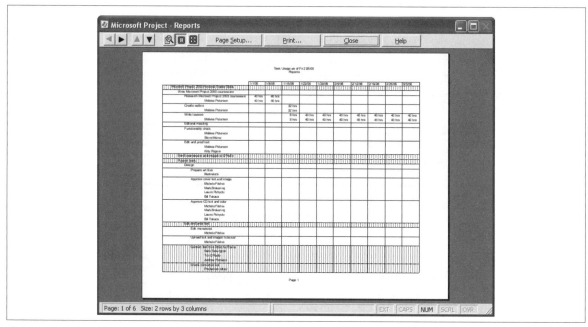

Figure 11-8. A preview of a Project report.

With so many different reports in Project, you will probably be able to find a report that is designed to compile the information you need. However, if you want to customize some of the finer details of a report, you can.

1 Select the Workload report category and click Select.

The Workload Reports dialog box appears. Notice the Task Usage report.

2 Select the Task Usage report and click the Edit button.

The Crosstab Report dialog box appears. You want to define report contents, so…

3 Click the Definition tab.

The Definition tab appears.

This is where you can choose what details you want to use to customize your report. The options available will vary depending on the report you're using, but the idea is the same.

To further define this report, let's highlight tasks that have not been completed.

4 Click the Filter list arrow and select Incomplete Tasks from the list. Click the Highlight checkbox.

Now the report will be filtered and highlighted for incomplete tasks.

Let's also view how much actual work has been done on these tasks.

5 Click the Work list arrow and select Actual Work from the list.

That's the only defining we'll do for now. Compare your dialog box to Figure 11-7.

6 Click OK.

You are returned to the Workload Reports dialog box.

Now, preview the Task Usage report to see how the definitions you added changed it.

7 Make sure the Task Usage report is selected, then click Select.

Your Task Usage report appears in Print Preview, as shown in Figure 11-8. Notice that all of the incomplete tasks are shaded, and actual work for the tasks appears in the chart cells.

8 Close the report preview and all open dialog boxes.

QUICK REFERENCE

TO DEFINE REPORT CONTENTS:

1. SELECT A REPORT AND CLICK THE EDIT BUTTON.

2. IF THE REPORT IS DEFINABLE, THE TASK REPORTS DIALOG BOX WILL APPEAR. (NOT ALL REPORTS ARE DEFINABLE.)

3. CLICK THE DEFINITION TAB.

4. DEFINE YOUR REPORT WITH THE OPTIONS IN THE DEFINITION TAB.

5. CLICK OK.

6. CLICK THE SELECT BUTTON TO PREVIEW YOUR DEFINED REPORT.

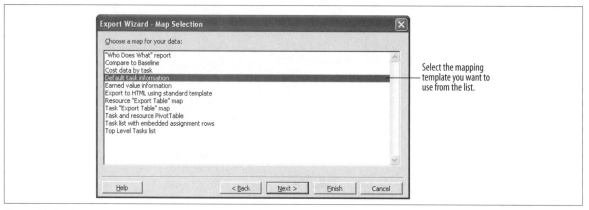

Figure 11-9. The Export Wizard – Map Selection dialog box.

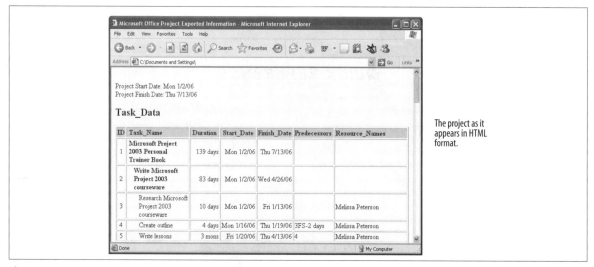

Figure 11-10. The web page version of the project in Internet Explorer.

You can save your project as a web page so that you can share your project information over the Internet or even a company's intranet. That way, the people involved with your project can view its information from anywhere in the world!

1 **Select** File → Save As Web Page **from the menu.**

The Save As dialog box appears.

Note the current location that's open; this is where the web page will be saved.

2 **Click the** Save button.

The Export Wizard appears. The wizard helps you specify what information you want to appear in the page, asks questions about what you want to do, automatically maps the fields in the project, and then allows you to verify the results.

⠿ NOTE ⠿ *A map simply identifies which information to include in a web page.*

3 **Click** Next.

If you're new to mapping information, or aren't sure what information you want to include in the web page, use an existing map.

4 Select the Use existing map **option and click** Next.

The Export Wizard – Map Selection dialog box appears, as shown in Figure 11-9.

Now, decide which map template you want to use.

5 Select the Default task information **option.**

If you were creating your own map for your data or wanted to further define the web page data, you could continue and click Next.

Since we're using a predefined map, we can skip ahead and finish the wizard.

6 Click the Finish button.

The dialog box closes, and the web page is saved in the location you specified.

To get an idea of what the report looks like as a web page, we've created and saved a web page report similar to the one you created in the previous steps. We'll use this file to see how the report looks as a web page.

7 Open your Internet browser program.

Internet Explorer will work best for viewing any type of web page file generated by a Microsoft program.

8 Select File → Open **from the menu. Click the** Browse button.

The Microsoft Internet Explorer dialog box appears.

Now, open the file from the Practice folder. (This is not the file you created in previous steps of this lesson).

9 Navigate to your Practice folder. Select the Project Personal Trainer **file and click** Open.

The HTML file appears in the browser, as shown in Figure 11-10.

10 Close the browser without saving any changes.

QUICK REFERENCE

TO SAVE A PROJECT AS A WEB PAGE:

1. SELECT FILE → SAVE AS WEB PAGE FROM THE MENU.

2. CLICK THE SAVE BUTTON.

3. FOLLOW THE EXPORT WIZARD AND ENTER THE REQUIRED INFORMATION.

4. CLICK FINISH.

Lesson Summary

Opening a Report

To Choose a Report Type: Select View → Reports from the menu, select a report category and click Select, and then select a report and click Select.

Adding Page Elements to a Report

To Add Page Elements to a Report: Open a report. In Print Preview, click the Page Setup button. In the Page Setup dialog box, use the various tabs to add page elements to your report.

Sorting a Report

To Sort a Report: Select a report and click the Edit button. If the report is sortable, the Task Reports dialog box will appear. Click the Sort tab, select your sorting options, and click OK. Click the Select button to preview your sorted report.

Defining Report Contents

To Define Report Contents: Select a report and click the Edit button. If the report is definable, the Task Reports dialog box will appear. Click the Definition tab, select your definition options, and click OK. Click the Select button to preview your defined report.

Saving a Project as a Web Page:

To Save a Project as a Web Page: Select File → Save As Web Page from the menu and click the Save button. Follow the Export Wizard and enter the required information, and then click Finish when you're done.

Quiz

1. Which of these is NOT a report category?
   A. Work Activities
   B. Costs
   C. Assignments
   D. Overview

2. The Custom button in the Reports dialog box doesn't contain predefined reports. (True or False?)

3. In some Project predefined reports, _____ is the only thing you can modify.
   A. text
   B. content
   C. workload
   D. page numbering

4. To open the Reports dialog box, go to _____ → _____.
   A. Format → Reports
   B. View → Reports
   C. Edit → Reports
   D. Project → Reports

5. You can choose to sort report information in _____ or _____ order.
   A. totalitarian or democratic
   B. ascending or descending
   C. alphabetical or numerical
   D. cost variation or work variation

6. Project offers you 22 _____ _____ to work with.
   A. report categories
   B. report formats
   C. predefined reports
   D. practice reports

7. Which of these Page Setup tabs is not accessible when you add page elements to a report?
   A. Legend
   B. Footers
   C. Margins
   D. Page

8. You can make changes to a report in Print Preview. (True or False?)

Homework

1. Navigate to your practice files and open the Homework 11 project file.

2. Select View → Reports from the menu to open the Reports dialog box and identify the five report category buttons. What does the sixth button do?

3. Format the text for the Cash Flow report so that all of the text is purple. The Cash Flow report is located in the Costs report category.

4. Define the Resource Usage report so that the time period is in days instead of weeks. The Resource Usage report is in the Workload report category.

5. Sort the Who Does What report so that it is sorted by ID, then by Baseline Finish, both in descending order. The Who Does What report is in the Assignment report category.

6. Add the baseline finish date to the footer in the "Tasks in Progress" report. The "Tasks in Progress" report is in the Current Activities report category.

7. View the Cash Flow report in Print Preview.

8. Close the Homework 11 file.

Quiz Answers

1. A. Work Activities is not a report category; the five report categories are: Overview, Current Activities, Costs, Assignments, and Workload.

2. True. The Custom button in the Reports dialog box does not contain predefined reports, because it is used to create new custom reports.

3. A. In some Project predefined reports, text is the only thing you can modify.

4. B. To open the Reports dialog box, go to View → Reports.

5. B. You can choose to sort report information in ascending or descending order.

6. C. Project offers you 22 predefined reports to work with.

7. A. The Legend and View tabs are not accessible when you add page elements to a report.

8. False. You can't make changes to a report in Print Preview.

CHAPTER 12

WORKING WITH MULTIPLE PROJECTS

CHAPTER OBJECTIVES:

Create a link between projects, Lesson 12.1

Consolidate a project, Lesson 12.2

View multiple project critical paths, Lesson 12.3

View consolidated project statistics, Lesson 12.4

Create a resource pool, Lesson 12.5

Prerequisites

- **Understand project management.**
- **Know how to perform basic Project functions.**

Single projects are the basis for project management, but sometimes it is necessary to view and work with multiple projects at the same time.

Fortunately, Project has features that enable you to observe and manage multiple open project files. This chapter will show you the most basic of these features, including consolidating project files and creating a shared resource pool.

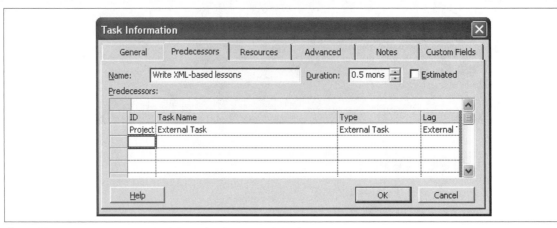

Figure 12-1. The Predecessors tab of the Task Information dialog box.

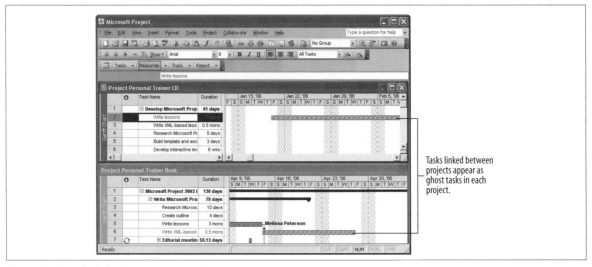

Figure 12-2. Tasks linked between two projects.

You can link tasks between projects, even if they are not consolidated. When you create task relationships across projects, keep in mind that the scheduling dates for predecessor tasks will impact the scheduling dates for successor tasks.

1 Navigate to your Practice folder, open the Lesson 12A file, and save this file as Project Personal Trainer Book. Open the Lesson 12B file and save it as Project Personal Trainer CD.

Let's link a task from the Project Personal Trainer CD file to a predecessor task in the Project Personal Trainer Book file.

2 Select Window → Project Personal Trainer CD from the menu. Select the Write XML-based lessons task.

Let's link this task to the "Write lessons" task #5 in the Project Personal Trainer Book file.

3 Click the 📄 Task Information button on the Standard toolbar.

The Task Information dialog box appears.

4 Click the Predecessors **tab.**

Now create the link by typing the project file name and the ID number of the predecessor task.

5 Click the first empty ID **field, type** Project Personal Trainer Book\5, **and press** Enter.

You have entered an external predecessor task link (the project name, backslash, ID number of the predecessor task) into the Predecessors tab, as shown in Figure 12-1.

6 Click OK.

The Task Information dialog box closes.

Notice that the "Write lessons" task becomes a ghost task in the Project Personal Trainer CD project. A *ghost task* is a placeholder for a task relationship. This means that the task relationship has been created between the task and a task within the project, but the task is not actually part of the project.

TIP

Double-clicking a ghost task will open the external file to which it belongs.

Let's view the task relationship in both projects at the same time.

7 Select Window → Arrange All **from the menu.**

The ghost tasks appear in both projects, as shown in Figure 12-2.

NOTE

You cannot update or make changes to ghost tasks; they can be modified only in their original projects.

QUICK REFERENCE

TO CREATE LINKS BETWEEN PROJECTS:

1. OPEN THE TWO PROJECT FILES BETWEEN WHICH YOU WANT TO CREATE A LINK.

2. SELECT THE TASK THAT YOU WANT TO DESIGNATE AS THE SUCCESSOR IN THE TASK RELATIONSHIP.

3. CLICK THE TASK INFORMATION BUTTON ON THE STANDARD TOOLBAR.

4. CLICK THE PREDECESSORS TAB.

5. CLICK THE ID FIELD. TYPE THE PROJECT NAME THAT CONTAINS THE PREDECESSOR TASK, A BACKSLASH, AND THEN THE ID NUMBER OF THE PREDECESSOR TASK. FOR EXAMPLE: Project Personal Trainer Book\5.

6. CLICK OK.

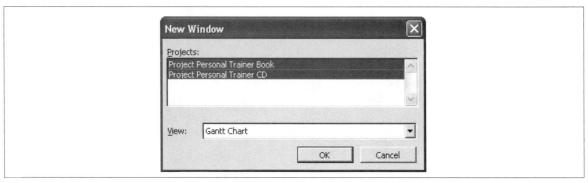

Figure 12-3. The New Window dialog box.

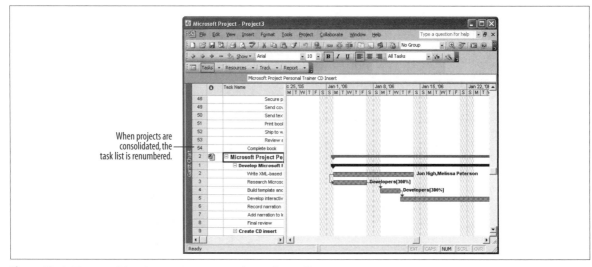

When projects are consolidated, the task list is renumbered.

Figure 12-4. The consolidated project in a new window and new file.

When you merge projects together, you create a *consolidated* project file. Consolidated projects allow you to piece together information to create an overall project plan or combine various projects into a master project plan. In this lesson, we will create a new consolidated project.

1 Make sure the Project Personal Trainer CD and Project Personal Trainer Book files are open.

Now, consolidate these projects in a new window.

2 Select Window → New Window from the menu.

The New Window dialog box appears, as shown in Figure 12-3. This is where you select the projects that

you want to consolidate in a new window and how you want to view them.

3 Select Project Personal Trainer Book, and then press and hold down the Shift key and select Project Personal Trainer CD. Make sure Gantt Chart appears in the View list and click OK. Close the Project Guide task pane.

Press the Shift or Ctrl key to select multiple files at a time.

Your new consolidated project window appears. Scroll down the window to see where the two projects were consolidated, as shown in Figure 12-4.

Each project that is consolidated in your new window is marked by a consolidated project icon in the indicator column.

4 Save the consolidated project as Project Personal Trainer Complete. **Do not save changes in other files.**

If what you really want to do is work with multiple projects at a time, create and save a workspace. Open the project files that you want to appear in your workspace, select File → Save Workspace, and save the workspace. Open the workspace to view the files opened in the workspace.

QUICK REFERENCE

TO CONSOLIDATE PROJECTS:

1. OPEN THE PROJECTS YOU WANT TO CONSOLIDATE.

2. SELECT WINDOW → NEW WINDOW FROM THE MENU.

3. IN THE NEW WINDOW DIALOG BOX, SELECT THE PROJECTS YOU WANT TO CONSOLIDATE.

4. CLICK OK.

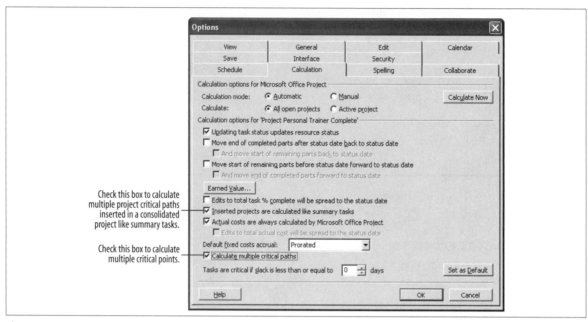

Check this box to calculate multiple project critical paths inserted in a consolidated project like summary tasks.

Check this box to calculate multiple critical points.

Figure 12-5. The Calculation tab of the Options dialog box.

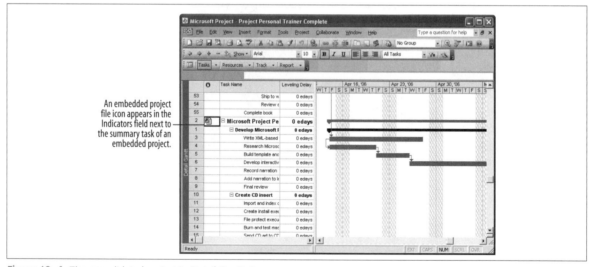

An embedded project file icon appears in the Indicators field next to the summary task of an embedded project.

Figure 12-6. The consolidated project in Detail Gantt view.

As you probably learned in the earlier stages of managing a Project file, it is important to monitor the critical path for a project. Likewise, it is important to keep an eye on multiple critical paths in a consolidated project, so you will be able to tell if adjustments made to the project plans will affect the critical paths. This lesson will teach you how to view multiple critical paths and then view the overall critical path across projects.

1 Select Tools → Options from the menu.

The Options dialog box appears.

2 Click the Calculation tab.

Next, choose to calculate multiple critical paths.

3 Check the Calculate multiple critical paths checkbox, as shown in Figure 12-5, and click OK.

Now let's view the multiple critical paths.

4 Select View → More Views from the menu.

The More Views dialog box appears. Find the Detail Gantt view.

5 Select the Detail Gantt view and click Apply.

Now you should be able to see the multiple critical paths, as shown in Figure 12-6.

6 Click the  Go To Selected Task button on the Standard toolbar.

Scroll down and to the right to see the critical paths of all the projects in this consolidated project. The projects are indicated by an embedded project icon in the summary task's Indicators field.

7 Select View → Gantt Chart from the menu.

The consolidated project appears in the default Gantt Chart view once again.

QUICK REFERENCE

TO VIEW CRITICAL PATHS FOR MULTIPLE PROJECTS:

1. OPEN A CONSOLIDATED PROJECT FILE.

2. SELECT TOOLS → OPTIONS FROM THE MENU.

3. CLICK THE CALCULATION TAB.

4. CHECK CALCULATE MULTIPLE CRITICAL PATHS AND CLICK OK.

5. SELECT VIEW → MORE VIEWS FROM THE MENU.

6. SELECT THE DETAIL GANTT VIEW AND CLICK APPLY.

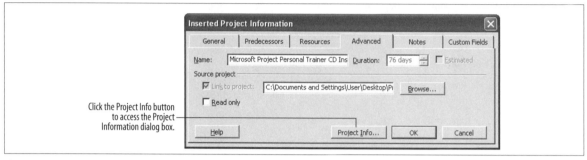

Click the Project Info button to access the Project Information dialog box.

Figure 12-7. The Advanced tab of the Inserted Project Information dialog box.

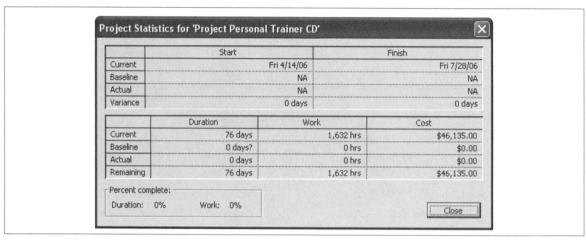

Figure 12-8. The Project Statistics dialog box.

Projects that are part of a consolidated project can still have their own information. You can view information for the entire consolidated project, but you can also view information for its individual embedded projects.

1 Select the Microsoft Project Personal Trainer CD Insert **summary task.**

This is the summary task for the second project in the consolidated project. You may have to scroll down to find this task.

Now let's view the subproject information.

2 Click the Task Information button **on the Standard toolbar.**

The Inserted Project Information dialog box appears.

3 Click the Advanced **tab.**

This tab shows you where the source file of your inserted project is, as shown in Figure 12-7.

⋮ NOTE ⋮ *You can make some changes in this tab. Uncheck the "Link to Project" checkbox to break the link between the inserted subproject and its source file; they will not update each other when changes are made in either one. Also, you can check the "Read only" checkbox to make the inserted subproject read-only in the master consolidated project; you won't be able to perform any actions on it or update it.*

4 Click the Project Info button **in the Inserted Project Information dialog box.**

The Project Information dialog box appears.

5 Click the Statistics button in the Project Information dialog box.

You have successfully viewed your inserted subproject information, as shown in Figure 12-8.

6 Close the Project Personal Trainer Complete file. Do not save changes to any of the files.

The consolidated project file is closed.

QUICK REFERENCE

TO VIEW INSERTED PROJECT INFORMATION:

1. OPEN A CONSOLIDATED PROJECT FILE.

2. SELECT THE SUMMARY TASK FOR THE INSERTED PROJECT.

3. CLICK THE TASK INFORMATION BUTTON ON THE STANDARD TOOLBAR.

4. CLICK THE ADVANCED TAB.

5. TO SEE ADDITIONAL INFORMATION, CLICK THE PROJECT INFO BUTTON AND THEN THE STATISTICS BUTTON.

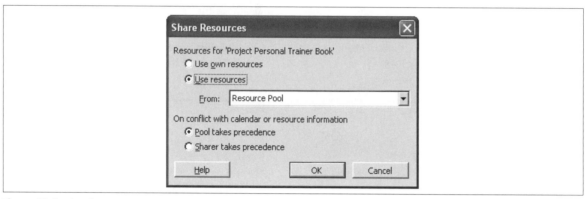

Figure 12-9. The Share Resources dialog box.

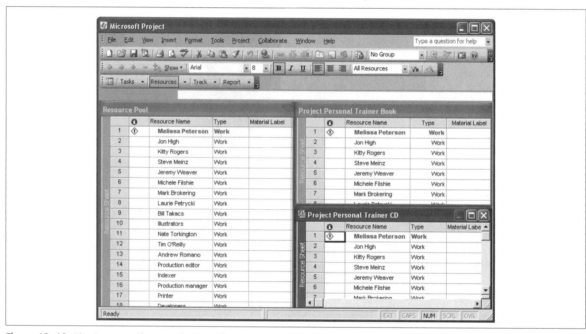

Figure 12-10. The Resource Sheets update to reflect the shared resources.

A *resource pool* is a collection of resources that can be shared among multiple projects. A resource pool allows you to schedule resources' work across projects, identify conflicts between assignments in different projects, and see how a resource's time is used in multiple projects. Each project that uses resources from the resource pool is called a *sharer file*.

The best way to create a resource pool is to create a new project file for the resource information—this makes it easier to manage resource information and task assignments between sharer files and the resource pool.

1 Create a new project file and save the file as Resource Pool.

This empty project file is where the resource pool will be saved.

2 Select View → Resource Sheet from the menu.

Repeat this step to view all open files in Resource Sheet view.

3 Repeat Step 2 to view the Project Personal Trainer Book and Project Personal Trainer CD files in Resource Sheet view.

This way you can see the resources as they are added to the resource pool.

4 Select Window → Arrange All from the menu.

The files are arranged in the window. Notice that there are some duplicate resources between the projects.

5 Select Window → Project Personal Trainer Book from the menu.

First, let's share the Project Personal Trainer Book resources in the Resource Pool.

6 Select Tools → Resource Sharing → Share Resources from the menu.

The Share Resources dialog box appears.

7 Click the Use Resources option. Click the From list arrow and select Resource Pool.

The Project Personal Trainer Book file will use resources from the selected file, Resource Pool.

The difference between the last two options in the dialog box is important.

- **Pool takes precedence:** Allows the resource pool file to overwrite information in the sharing file.
- **Sharer takes precedence:** Allows the sharing file to overwrite information in the resource pool and other sharing files.

We'll use the default option, "Pool takes precedence," for now. Compare your dialog box to Figure 12-9.

8 Click OK to close the Share Resources dialog box.

The resources from the Project Personal Trainer Book file have been added to the Resource Pool file.

Now, add the resources from the Project Personal Trainer CD to the Resource Pool.

9 Select Window → Project Personal Trainer CD from the menu.

Add this project's resource to the resource pool.

10 Select Tools → Resource Sharing → Share Resources from the menu.

The Share Resources dialog box appears.

11 Click the Use Resources option. Make sure Resource Pool appears in the From box. Click OK.

The resources are added to the Resource Pool, as shown in Figure 12-10.

Notice that one of the resources is overallocated in the Resource Pool. When resources are shared, all their assignment information is shared between the projects. As you can see in this instance, the Melissa Peterson resource must be assigned to tasks at the same time between the projects.

12 Close all files without saving changes.

QUICK REFERENCE

TO CREATE A RESOURCE POOL FOR MULTIPLE PROJECTS:

1. OPEN THE PROJECT(S) WITH THE RESOURCES YOU WANT TO SHARE IN THE RESOURCE POOL.

2. CREATE A NEW PROJECT FILE AND SAVE THE FILE AS "RESOURCE POOL".

3. SELECT THE PROJECT FILE WITH THE RESOURCES THAT YOU WANT TO SHARE IN THE RESOURCE POOL.

4. SELECT TOOLS → RESOURCE SHARING → SHARE RESOURCES FROM THE MENU.

5. SELECT THE USE RESOURCES OPTION.

6. CLICK THE FROM LIST ARROW AND SELECT THE RESOURCE POOL, AND THEN CLICK OK.

7. REPEAT THESE STEPS TO ADD ADDITIONAL RESOURCES TO THE RESOURCE POOL.

Lesson Summary

Creating Links Between Projects

To Create Links Between Projects: Open the two project files you want to create a link between. Select the task that you want to designate as the successor in the task relationship. Click the Task Information button on the Standard toolbar, and then click the Predecessors tab. Click the ID field and type the project name that contains the predecessor task, a backslash, and then the ID number of the predecessor task (for example, Project Personal Trainer Book\5). Click OK.

Consolidating Projects

To Consolidate Projects: Open the projects that you would like to consolidate. Select Window → New Window from the menu. In the New Window dialog box, select the projects you want to consolidate and click OK.

Viewing Multiple Project Critical Paths

You must create a consolidated project before you can view multiple critical paths.

To View Multiple Project Critical Paths: Open a consolidated project file, select Tools → Options from the menu, and then click the Calculation tab. Check the Cal-culate multiple critical paths checkbox and click OK. Select View → More Views from the menu, select the Detail Gantt view, and then click Apply.

Viewing Consolidated Project Statistics

To View Inserted Project Information: Open a consolidated project file, and then select the summary task for the inserted project. Click the Task Information button and click the Advanced tab. To see additional information, click the Project Info button and then the Statistics button.

Creating a Resource Pool

To Create a Resource Pool for Multiple Projects: Open the project(s) with the resources you want to share in the resource pool. Create a new project file and save the file as "Resource Pool". Select the project file with the resources that you want to share in the resource pool, and select Tools → Resource Sharing → Share Resources from the menu. Select the Use Resources option. Click the From list arrow and select the Resource Pool, and then click OK. Repeat to add additional resources to the Resource Pool.

Quiz

1. To organize open project files on your screen, select Window → ____.

   A. Order All

   B. View All

   C. Organize All

   D. Arrange All

2. Light-gray tasks that are linked across projects are called ____ tasks.

   A. ghost

   B. zombie

   C. ghoul

   D. spooky

3. A resource pool project file has tasks in it. (True or False?)

4. After you insert projects into a consolidated file, you can still access each of the projects separately. (True or False?)

5. In which tab of the Options dialog box can you change multiple critical path options?

   A. Tab key

   B. General tab

   C. Calculation tab

   D. Edit tab

Homework

1. Start Microsoft Project 2003.

2. Navigate to your Practice folder and open the Homework 12A and Homework 12B project files.

3. Arrange the two projects you have open on your screen.

4. Link task #13, "Sell lemon bars at stand," in Homework 12B to a predecessor task, task #15, "Dye the dog lemon yellow," in Homework 12A.

5. Create a resource pool between Homework 12A and Homework 12B.

6. Create a new consolidated project with Homework 12A and Homework 12B.

7. View all of the multiple critical paths in your new "Lemonade" consolidated project.

8. Close the project files without saving any changes.

Quiz Answers

1. D. To organize open project files on your screen, select Window → Arrange All.

2. B. Light-gray tasks that are linked across projects are called ghost tasks.

3. False. A resource pool project file only has resources in it.

4. True. After you insert projects into a consolidated file, you can still access each project separately.

5. C. The Calculation tab of the Options dialog box is where you can change multiple critical path options.

INDEX

Colophon

Our look is the result of reader comments, our own experimentation, and feedback from distribution channels. Distinctive covers complement our distinctive approach to technical topics, breathing personality and life into potentially dry subjects.

Genevieve d'Entremont was the production editor and copyeditor for *Project 2003 Personal Trainer*. Sarah Sherman proofread the book. Sanders Kleinfeld and Claire Cloutier provided quality control. Julie Hawks wrote the index.

The cover image of the comic book hero is an original illustration by Brian Kong.

Emma Colby designed and produced the cover of this book with Adobe InDesign CS and Photoshop CS. The typefaces used on the cover are Base Twelve, designed by Zuzana Licko and issued by Emigre, Inc., and JY Comic Pro, issued by AGFA Monotype.

Melanie Wang designed the interior layout. Karen Montgomery designed the CD label. This book was converted by Keith Fahlgren to FrameMaker 5.5.6 with a format conversion tool created by Erik Ray, Jason McIntosh, Neil Walls, and Mike Sierra that uses Perl and XML technologies. The typefaces are Minion, designed by Robert Slimbach and issued by Adobe Systems; Base Twelve and Base Nine; JY Comic Pro; and TheSansMono Condensed, designed by Luc(as) de Groot and issued by LucasFonts.

The technical illustrations that appear in the book were produced by Robert Romano, Jessamyn Read, and Lesley Borash, using Macromedia FreeHand MX and Adobe Photoshop CS.